Full English Breakfast

Full English Breakfast

A Ramble Through London, Wales, and Yorkshire: Travel, Adventures, and History

Todd Wisti

Writers Club Press
San Jose New York Lincoln Shanghai

Full English Breakfast
A Ramble Through London, Wales, and Yorkshire:
Travel, Adventures, and History

Writers Club Press
an imprint of iUniverse.com, Inc.

For information address:
iUniverse.com, Inc.
5220 S 16th, Ste. 200
Lincoln, NE 68512
www.iuniverse.com

Every attempt has been made by the author to include accurate and fair accounts
of the travel, adventures, and history that are included within these pages.
Reviews and recommendations are those of the author's personal preferances,
and are reflective of his experiences at the establishments mentioned.

ISBN: 0-595-19196-7

Printed in the United States of America

"Yes, I'm away tomorrow, Mr. Summergill."
"Tomorrow, eh?" he raised his eyebrows.
"Yes, to London. Ever been there?"
James Herriot (1916–1995)—*All Things Bright and Beautiful*

Contents

Foreword (by Bill Wisti)

As do many people worldwide, I consider travel to be one of life's little pleasures. However, some who know me well might argue that point and tell you that I have an almost compulsive need to travel. They might be right....

England has always been at the top of my list when I begin to think about places I'd rather be, and, given half a minute to think about it, I'll have a bag packed and will be on the next flight to the British Isles. I've always found the proprietors of any of the thousands of B&B's which Great Britain has to offer to be gracious and kind, showing concern for the comfort and well being of their guests, and, within five minutes of arrival, I'll invariably hear the following: "You *will* have the Full English Breakfast in the morning?"

England...it's good to be back!

Acknowledgements

Thanks to Cynthia Pacheco and to Bill Wisti for lending their eyes to the manuscript, and to Bill, also, for not minding if I tagged along.

Prologue

When I'm at home, I'll make a quick weekday dive into a bowl of breakfast cereal in the morning, after a mug or two of hot coffee. Sometimes I'll include a buttered slice of toast with my breakfast and, on occasion, I'll take a sausage out of the freezer and pop it into the microwave for a minute to liven up the morning meal. Sadie and Gridley, the two dogs that have been hanging out at the house for the past several years, are always more than appreciative to receive a bowl of dry dog food apiece, along with any of my breakfast sustenance I feel too full to eat. Claire, the cat who came to be a part of the household, also, many years ago, has an equally humdrum meal of dry cat food. But we are used to the routine, and we are all too fixed in these morning rituals to change at this point (at least I am).

On weekends, I'll attempt, on occasion, to recreate my favorite full English breakfasts. Somehow, my efforts at this art don't match up or taste the same as what can be enjoyed at the bed and breakfasts in Britain. Possibly it's because I don't have the same ingredients readily available to me as are obtainable in Britain, or maybe I don't have the appropriate tableware, or perhaps I don't have the knack or patience for cooking up a morning meal with all the trimmings: eggs, sausages, tomatoes, mushrooms, bacon, toast, tea, and coffee, as well as also setting out a generous selection of fruits, juices, and condiments.

I'm not much of a breakfast man at home, but put me in Britain, and I could grow fat on what is offered, if it wasn't for the tremendous amount of sightseeing and rambling to be done.

A ramble can be a wandering narrative, and it can also be a leisurely excursion, taking in the pleasures of the land and the peoples of the region, and enjoying every minute of it (well, almost). In November 2000 I rambled through London, Cardiff, and Yorkshire with my older, bearded brother, Bill. Bill is a wizened traveler, being more than a dozen years older than myself and having taken many more excursions to England than I have. Throughout this trip, I learned bits and snatches of British history and customs and, in the process, ate my share of nourishing breakfasts.

CHAPTER ONE

A Long Anticipated Outing

The waiter glanced sideways, and nodded in my direction as he conferred with the other staff members inside the kitchen. I had obviously caused a fair amount of distress at the time I made my brazen request at the breakfast table. Now I was getting nervous, as the staff gathered in a small group conference, each of them giving me a quick look coupled with horrified grimaces as they discussed their situation. The expressions I received held astonishment and maybe just the tiniest amount of antipathy.

The kitchen was easily viewable from my seat, and as I looked across the breakfast room I met the piercing gaze of my waiter's eyes; I offered an apologetic smile, which I hoped he wouldn't mistake for haughtiness. My brother, Bill, sat across from me, and he was not able to witness the council taking place on the kitchen side of the breakfast room.

Time seemed to drag on. I spooned corn flakes into my mouth as I took inventory of my surroundings: it was a fairly large room, with a dozen or so tables neatly arranged in the tastefully decorated scrubbed environs; carefully arranged china, silverware and napkins graced the tables, and there were several other breakfast customers enjoying their morning meals. An open door leading to a small garden helped to circulate the air of a fresh, cool, late autumn English morning.

As one walks into the breakfast room, a bar of cereals, fruit, milk, fresh coffee, and assorted condiments lends an invitation to make one's self at home, and to tuck into the offerings. After gathering the first course, and soon after sitting down to look over the menu standing upright on each table, a waiter or waitress stops by to ask which menu items the customer prefers. Toast, eggs, bacon, Cumberland sausages, tomatoes, and mushrooms are all possibilities for the breakfast plate. "Everything" is certainly a valid response when the server asks what one would like to order. Ice water is not on the menu, and, possibly, I should not have asked for it.

I saw another staff member join the kitchen group's discussion. I heard her let out a quick gasp and say, "He wanted what?" "*Shh!*" she was told. They all looked at me again, as did the whole of the other breakfast patrons. I was trapped. A hushed order was given, the conference broke up, and the staff scattered. Soon, a slightly out of breath server set before me a glass filled with sparkling clear water and, in the glass, two dainty ice cubes.

"Thank you." I offered. But there was no time for the server to respond. She was, I'm sure, rushing off to the nearest employment office to look for work which did not have anything to do with dealing with unreasonable requests by Americans.

I wouldn't have guessed that asking for ice water with my breakfast would release such an outpouring of emotions, much less cause an entire stoppage of everyone else's meal at this London bed and breakfast. I was outstandingly tense as this conference had been in session. Truly I was. I half-supposed the proprietors of the B&B would walk up to the table and ask me to return to my room, pack my belongings, and leave at once. Or possibly my presence would be requested in the kitchen in order for me to make a formal apology to the staff for my actions. Or maybe, and this is where I gasp, I would be informed that ice costs extra.

I made a mental note to make an attempt to not ask for ice water with my full English breakfast again. After all, I don't mind keeping on the kitchen staff's good side.

On the other hand, maybe something I should try the next time I'm feeling a little spirited is to once again ask for ice water with a meal. But, when I receive the glass of ice water I could look at it, tilt my head sideways, close an eye halfway, *really* study the glass hard, sigh, and ask the server, "If it's not much trouble, could I have just one more ice cube, please?" No. I could never do that. Well, maybe.

Bill and I had arrived in England less than twenty-four hours earlier, before this breakfast vagary, on a seasonable November day, which had offered clear skies, cloudy skies, cool temperatures, as well as rain thrown in to round out the mix. My older brother, Bill, makes it a point to spend a little time in England at least a couple times a year. Me, I rarely leave my neighborhood, so this was really a treat, not only to be out of the neighborhood, but out of my Minnesota town, the Midwest, the U.S., and North America. Change can be good. It makes a person see things in a new light. Such as ice cubes.

It was a long anticipated outing. I had made a short trip to Britain over two years beforehand, as I tagged along on one of Bill's trips. It seems like I used to do a little bit of tagging along when I was a kid, too. That's one thing about older brothers; whether it's taking a trip to the store or going halfway across the world, there can be a younger sibling whining, "Can I come with?" Now, nearly forty years after my first tagalong, I was tagging along once again, and my use of prepositions and my various other abusages can still leave something to be desired.

We had purchased the plane tickets for our November flight during a summer fare sale, while the airlines were beginning to book their flights for Britain's off-season. It was August when we bought the tickets and began to plan our trip. Now, from August to November, that can be a horrifically long time when all a person wants to do is get on with a vacation. I'm afraid there may have even been a wasted minute or two at my place of work, where I sat at my desk and drifted off, imagining myself in some old smoky public house, next to a crackling fire, warming myself from the cool, rainy evening, and reviving my spirits with a pint or two of the house's finest hand pulled cask conditioned ale. A pair of toothsome barmaids would sit on either side of me, and listen to my tales of tramping though the English countryside, damp and hungry; they would pat me on the shoulders, whisper *there, there*, and offer to make me a sandwich.

I had tall expectations for this vacation.

Throughout late summer and into mid-autumn, Bill and I regularly exchanged e-mails and we proposed itineraries to one another. Our flight landed at Gatwick Airport, just thirty minutes from London, so it would only be right to spend a few days in London.

At the first thought of spending even a day or two in London, I had misgivings: everybody, it seems, wants to see London when a journey is made to England; I was more interested in visiting some of the smaller, quieter cities and towns. However, after doing some poking around in library books and on the Internet, I discovered that I, too, was eager to spend at least a few days in London. Big Ben, Westminster Abbey, red double-decker busses, the River Thames, and the Tower of London all called out to me.

Bill's plans in England included some business, which would be done in the old walled city of York, a couple hundred miles north of London. On my prior visit to Britain, I had flown into Glasgow, Scotland, and York was as far south as I had explored. I like that medieval cobbled city, York, and I was agreeable to spend a couple days there, taking in some old haunts, and making it a northern leg to this trip.

After York, we would plan on heading west, towards Liverpool and Chester, then through Wales for a short tour before returning south and back to London.

Our plans were as set in stone as we wanted to make them, and that means that neither one of us had a firm rota, but nevertheless we agreed on cities to visit and an approximate circular route that would get us to our intended locales.

When we arrived at the Minneapolis-St. Paul International airport, we discovered, as we checked in, that our 4:20 PM flight had just been cancelled. Luckily though, there was an exact same plane, leaving at exactly the same time, making the exact same connection that the airline would let us ride in. Now if that isn't generosity, I don't know what is.

We boarded the plane, pulled away from the gate, and there we sat. And sat. And sat. And sat. We were to make a connecting flight in St. Louis, Missouri, but some late autumn thunderstorms in Missouri were snarling the St. Louis airport up, and we had to wait our turn to get up in the air. Why the people who board the passengers don't check on these things beforehand is mystifying, but what are you going to do?

In St. Louis there was an uneventful wait for the connecting flight. Uneventful, that is, except for leisurely walks though the concourse, and marveling at the smoking lounges, which are glass cubes, a little larger than a compact car, and seem expandable to take in as many as possibly several scores of chain smokers. Haling from Minnesota, I was intrigued to see that it was physically possible for a person to smoke inside a building, although somewhat uncomfortably, it seems.

Once on the flight from St. Louis and towards London there was some sort of, hmmm… what did they call it? Oh yes! "Dinner." I had what was featured as "Mexican Chicken." It was, to the best of my knowledge, "chicken." This was probably some de-beaked old hen who had given her life to laying soft shelled eggs in an enclosure barely large enough to sneeze in, and this was the thanks she got: being marinated in salt and "Mexican spices," then served on board an airplane to someone who had purchased a discounted ticket. Thinking I might appease my appetite some, I put the old hen aside and scooped up a forkful of rice; it was as if I had a mouthful of softened plastic pellets. I tucked into my meal the best I could, watched some movie that really never held my interest as much as the crying baby did, who was only a few seats away. What a jolly way to travel to England.

Nearing Gatwick, I was impressed. I had grown used to the dead, brown, dry frozen grass of the upper Midwest that had begun appearing in September. As the plane dipped down closer to Earth, I saw lush, green grass, alive with vibrancy. We seemed to be flying over a multitude of golf courses. I saw expanses of the green fields, with what seemed like an extraordinary amount of golf balls lost to the greens.

It was only after several more minutes that I realized we were still a ways away from the ground, and what I thought were golf balls were actually sheep. Now why was I thinking that I'd be able to see a golf ball on the ground from hundreds of feet in the air, when I can't even find one after I've managed a lucky shot on a course and actually had a ball travel more than five feet in the forward direction? The duration of the flight was weighing heavily on my senses.

Throughout the plane's descent, the baby cried. I started feeling sorry for the little critter. It's hard for anyone to be packaged up in a metal cylinder and shot halfway across the planet; even more so, it seems, for a baby. The change in air pressure must be uncomfortable, as well as horrifying for a tiny body.

The plane landed at Gatwick and I was still feeling a little pity for the tiny cherub who had put up with so much inner turmoil throughout the flight. Bill had packed lightly, and had only his carry-on bag, but I had one checked-in bag to pick up. As I waited to pick up my bag, I listened to a salty philippic from a tattooed American youth with ripped jeans, stylish piercings, and a fine black leather jacket who was attempting to engage in lively banter with a chum with whom he had obviously traveled.

"That dang-blasted little ding-dong rascal was sitting right in back of me and cried the *whole* gosh-darn flight!" he lamented about the fate he had suffered over the past eight hours. His acerbic words pushed the upper volume limit of his voice, and have, of course, been slightly tidied up for those who are of a nervous disposition.

The youth's companion stared straight ahead.

"Golly, that was awful!" the youth emphasized for good measure.

The young man and his friend found their bags and took off at breakneck speed, and suddenly I felt mad, too, and relayed my emotions to Bill, who got exercised as well. I picked up my bag, and we stepped up our pace to match the speed of Gatwick's moving sidewalks.

Now, in my day, I wore torn jeans (not for style, though, they just happened to rip), a pretty cool black leather jacket, pierced an ear, and got a tattoo or two, but I'd be hard pressed to have a childish outburst like that in a public place. I might have been more prone to lay it on the line in a way such as, oh, I don't know... by drawing a breath in, shaking my head, and muttering, "*Shit!*" Which would, I'm sure, have been met with healthy approval from anyone who had been on that flight and within earshot.

CHAPTER TWO

The Address is London

Passport Control has an irksome line of restless people that queues out forever, while a traveler waits to answer a few questions brought on by a uniformed agent about who one is, how long one will be staying in the country, and the address at which one intends to stay. That last question, when posed to me, left me flummoxed. I had no idea where I would be residing over the next few days. Bill and I hadn't gotten far enough into our plans yet to know exactly where we'd be lodging. I told the gent that I supposed I would be sleeping at a bed and breakfast, but that there were no reservations for any particular one as of yet; he was looking for something slightly more concrete. After a friendly discussion, he said that he'd just write down my address as "London." I was relieved that I would now have a proper place to call my home for the next few days, even though it was somewhat on the generic side.

Unfortunately, after that, the customs agent hit me up with an inquiry that I had least expected. It was only days away from the year

2000 presidential election, and the agent asked me whom I favored to be the next president of the United States.

I hemmed and hawed between the two major candidates, not only trying to put names with those faces I could see in my head, but also trying to remember who I had checked off for my vote on the proxy ballot that I had mailed in to the county offices before this trip. It was nearly hopeless, until (at last) I remembered one of the names, and blurted it out, blaming my slow moving brain on the long flight, and explaining that I was having quite a time trying to think of anything, much less presidential candidates, at the time. He let me pass into his country without further interrogation.

Bill and I made our way to the Gatwick Express train platform. I had heard that a ticket for the train may be purchased either at the ticket window or on the train itself. Buying a ticket on the train sounded almost too good to be true, as there would be no need to stand in line at a ticket counter. Being a little on the skeptical side, I chose to stand in a queue to buy a ticket. That was a fortunate decision, it turned out, as there was a confused woman with an eastern European accent looking for assistance on how to buy a train ticket. She turned to me to ask my advice. This might typically be a bad move for anyone, asking me for advice on how something works. Nine times out of ten, I'll get at least half the explanation wrong, and I won't realize it until we've parted ways.

"You just stand in this line, and when you get up to the ticket clerk, say that you'd like to buy a ticket."

She thanked me wholeheartedly, and I was immensely gratified that there weren't any tough follow up questions, such as, "Thanks for your help! Say, you sound American. Who do you think will win the presidential election?"

Bill purchased his Gatwick Express ticket at the window, also. After I acquired my ticket, I compared it to Bill's, and noticed that my ticket was a little different than Bill's was. We studied the two tickets, and Bill posed to me, "I bought a round trip ticket. Why didn't you get one?

Aren't you planning on going back home next week?" I hadn't thought of inquiring about round trip tickets. That seemed like it would have been a good idea, especially once I realized that they are discounted compared to buying two single trip tickets.

Reaching the platform for the Gatwick Express, we thought our luck was great. Here, waiting for us, was a Gatwick Express train, about to leave for London's Victoria Station. Or was it? It could be, but if this wasn't the right train, where would we end up? There were only seconds to spare, and no time for hesitation. This was not a good recipe for two cloudy jet lagged brains. We hesitated, the conductor's whistle blew, and the train chugged away without us. It was, of course, the correct train.

This was not a problem, though. The Gatwick Express trains run frequently, the temperature wasn't bad, and this was a nice chance to stand outside, take in the English scenery and have a long awaited breath of fresh air. There was some concrete to look at, a few parked cars, some asphalt, a fence or two, more concrete, and a man walking from a block of concrete to a car. I scanned the scenery a few more times to make sure I hadn't missed anything. No, that seemed to be about it.

The next Gatwick Express finally arrived. We bounded on to it with transport.

I liked that Gatwick Express train ride into London. I had never been on a real train before, one that was actually going someplace. Once, I had been on a summer tourist excursion train in Duluth, Minnesota, touring past the shipyards into Superior, Wisconsin, into the Wisconsin woods for a few minutes, then back again to Duluth after three quarters of an hour. This was different, though. We were heading from Point "A" to a Point "B." And Point "B" was Victoria Station.

It was a half-hour train ride, through the graffiti covered suburbs of London (and the closer we got towards the city the more colorful the graffiti became). A conductor came through to check for passengers' tickets, and to let passengers purchase a ticket if needed (so it was true that this would happen!), and an attendant arrived with a trolley full of refreshments for purchase if one can't wait for arrival at the rail station to get nourished. There weren't many people riding in this particular car, but a good number of the passengers that were there took the attendant up on the offer to buy a snack or a beverage for immediate gratification. I was fine with looking out the window to take in the view of the ever-changing scenery.

Victoria Station was not quite what I thought it would be. It's a nice old building, and I was under the impression that it was a train station, and a train station only. After disembarking from the train, I found that it's also a shopping mall and a tube stop. Well, why not? The roof leaks a bit, and pigeons fly around inside. Much to my surprise, there were people walking around who were smoking in an enclosed environment. By gosh, a place like this in Minnesota would cause a spasm to the ones who believe that a clean, sterile environment is the only way to live. In a fit of support for the English way of life, I sidestepped a pigeon or two, dodged a few puddles, and made an attempt to look not too much like a tourist, although my wheeled suitcase and gawking around most likely gave me away.

Bill led the way though Victoria Station, up an escalator, and past the stores in the mall, after which we went down a sloping floor in the mall that led us to a sidewalk outdoors. Yes, I was finally taking in the London air! Funny, but it didn't smell that much different than the air back home in Minneapolis. A little bit of traffic fumes, a small whiff of green grass and trees, some cigarette smoke, maybe a scant scent of old garbage. Every now and then, though, there is a certain palpable scent that pops up. I can't put my finger on it. It smells… old. It's not really musty, and it's not a bad smell, though some may term it acrid. It's a smell that might emit from a city after it's been around for a couple thousand years. It causes the senses to tingle, and makes a person feel like he is somewhere where there is an abundance of history.

Londinium is the name the ancient Romans gave to this city after invading Britain in the first century AD. As the years passed, Roman city walls were built, Vikings raided, William the Conqueror conquered, London Bridges were built, replaced, and rebuilt, the plagues called for people to bring out their dead, Shakespeare produced plays at the Globe Theatre, and the city survived the Great Fire of 1666. To jump further ahead, there was Queen Victoria, Winston Churchill, the swinging London scene of the 1960's, the punk rock scene of the 1970's, and, of course, Princess Diana.

I'm not sure what it is, exactly, that is in the air that causes the nose to sniff out and explore this singular tang. My bet would be that it is either the remnants of the plague, or the musty smell of aging punk rockers, but I could be wrong. It could very well be the scent of coal warming peoples' homes.

It's fortunate that someone decided that it would be a good idea to paint little arrows at the crosswalks in this neighborhood to tell people which way to look for cars before crossing the street. As much as I tell myself to first look right before crossing the street, invariably I'll forget. The notices on the pavement are a good reminder not to get run over by an oncoming vehicle.

We toted our suitcases for a good ten or fifteen minutes, and took note of a blue plaque on a building that told of Winston Churchill once having lived in this neighborhood; we arrived at a bed and breakfast that Bill had stayed at on one of his previous London visits. We buzzed the doorbell to get into the lobby of the Georgian House Hotel, and we found that an *en-suite* room was available for two nights, but after that the hotel was booked full. We were planning on three nights in London, before taking off to other parts of Britain, but we decided to book the available room for two nights, and then take our chances at whatever place we could find for the third night.

Checking into the B&B was a quick and easy procedure (especially since Bill took charge of it). We headed up several flights of stairs to find our room and unpack, stow our valuables away in the room's safe, and figure out what we'd do to amuse ourselves the rest of the afternoon. Of course, we both had a look at the en-suite section of our lodgings. En-suite means that there is a shower, sink, and a toilet available in the accommodation, and not down the hall. En-suite was there, and we were satisfied. The Georgian House is a pleasant place, I decided.

After settling ourselves in, we took a walk around the Victoria neighborhood. It didn't take too much marching around before we came across a street sign that advertised itself as Buckingham Palace Road. Thinking that it might be long walk to get to Buckingham Palace, but without any better plans for the afternoon, we set out to find it. And there it was, Buckingham Palace, only a few blocks up the road, looking finer, larger and prettier than any picture that I had ever laid eyes on. We took our cameras out and snapped some pictures by the big metal gates, and marveled at the surroundings.

We were there at just the right time to take in a miniature changing of the guards. This wasn't the full-fledged pageantry that we've all heard so much about. For the real changing of the guards, I've heard that you have to get to Buckingham Palace early to see much of anything, then wait around forever, and sometimes they choose not to have the ceremony if there are circumstances beyond control, such as if the weather isn't cooperating just so.

This was a good little display. A few guards stamping about, looking mighty regal, and then going on to their respective duties. I think they might have been having a shift change for a toilet break.

As an American, I feel a little uncomfortable at times asking for the toilet. The word itself seems a little harsh. Toilet. "I need to use the toilet." "Where's your toilet?" "Is there a toilet nearby?" Like so many other Americans, I've grown accustomed to asking for the rest room. However, I don't really want to rest in a room (although sometimes that would be nice to do). I want to use a toilet. The word "toilet" is straightforward, and a better way to phrase having to expel bodily waste than other ways that could be mentioned. (Although "water closet" and "loo" are not bad, either.) Though I didn't need to use a toilet at the time we were at Buckingham Palace, if I did have to I would have, with only slight hesitation, asked where a toilet is located.

As the afternoon light grew dim, we found a string of stores, including a discount bookstore that I decided would be a nice place in which to soak up some English civility. There was a good selection of books that I wanted to buy and take home, and an impressive assortment of compact discs, too. After careful consideration of books on gardening, football, travel in England's countryside, and compact discs by the likes of the Troggs and other greats, I noticed Bill standing by the door, looking like he was ready to travel on to other sights. I'm not sure how long we were in the store, but it was probably a long time, and obviously too long for Bill's tastes.

As a rule, I have an aversion to shopping. But, put me in a bookstore or in a purveyor of sound recordings, and I can get lost for a day unless there's someone to drag me out of there. Bill was ready to drag me out of the bookstore, I'm sure. As I walked towards the front door, where Bill was standing, his voice dropped an octave and took on a gravel-like tone as he suggested, "Well, it starting to rain, we'd better go."

I was still hours off from making my choice of purchases, and there were most likely other discount book stores in England that I could visit another time, plus I was in favor of walking in a bit of London rain, so I countered, "O.K., I'm ready."

Although it was still early in the evening, we were both becoming more than a little hungry. We walked around the neighborhood to look at the menus of several likely establishments, and, in the process, I got an outstanding rap on the noggin by a woman who was more intent on opening her umbrella rather than being concerned for any bystanders whom her umbrella might likely impale. I spotted a man with a produce cart who stood, determined in his work, with a grimacing stare as he waited out the cold rain for the time his next customer would arrive.

We wound up back at Victoria Station for dinner. There we found a restaurant called Garfunkle's, which we thought would satisfy our dining needs completely. Garfunkle's is a clean place, with plenty of seating at the time we were there. Bill tried the fish and chips, and I had sausages, mash, and peas. It was an uneventful meal, except for trying to catch the waitress's attention when we wanted something, such as ordering our meal, or attempting to pay our bill. We had wandered into a chain restaurant, which had not too much charm, and even less of a beer menu. While we were seated, we noticed a place across the way that advertised draught Guinness. Rats. A hearty Guinness with a foamy head would have been mighty tasty.

I resigned myself to the fact that I would have to wait until another time to enjoy the frothy wholesomeness of a genuine pub beer, as we both opted to have a look around in a couple stores, then head back to the B&B for an early evening to hopefully combat a little bit of jet lag.

On our walk back to the B&B, and while I decided whether or not to cross a busy intersection as the traffic light was about to change from green to red, Bill had the fortitude to jump into the crosswalk and invent a merry little jig while caught between the eastbound and westbound streams of traffic. A car horn or two beeped, adding to the excitement, and providing a bit of musical accompaniment to his show. If I had thought of it at the time, I would have offered a round of applause in appreciation for the evening's performance.

Back in our room, and settling down for the night, I tried a cup of tea while watching the television. The complimentary teabags that were set out by the B&B's staff had sort of an off taste once brewed and sipped. *Soap*, I thought at first, then I had the notion that this might be some sort of flower-flavored tea. The wrapping of the teabag didn't hold much of a clue as to the ingredients. The tea was not really what I had expected, but there were no other choices except for freeze-dried coffee, which I later found to be somewhat strange tasting, also.

The television had an interesting quiz show on, "The Weakest Link." Fast-fired questions by Anne Robinson, who, according to the TV listings "sneers at a few more contestants." The program was entertaining and there's a chance that I'd watch this English program on occasion if it was on in the States.

CHAPTER THREE

Tubes, Beatles, Lowbrows

I had a bit of jet lag on the first morning in London. I was awake at 3:30 AM. Much too early. I attempted to tell myself that this was the wee hours of the morning, but my brain refused to cooperate, so I passed the time by cooking up a batch of more of that flowery-tasting tea, munching on a few cookies, and ruminating over the news in the previous day's *Evening Standard* newspaper. As I was about to drift back into slumber, I noted in a newspaper article that flu jabs were becoming available. Basking in the reassuring fact that I had received my winter flu shot a couple weeks beforehand, I fell asleep for a couple more hours of needed respite.

After waking up at a later, more reasonable hour, showering, and having caused a commotion about my asking for ice water with my morning meal, Bill and I made our way to the Victoria tube station. We queued at the ticket window, and found that for £3.90 a person can ride all day in zones one and two on the Underground, which pretty much encompasses everywhere a typical tourist would want to take in during a day. The tube fares are sequestered into zones: zone one is the inner circle of London and Westminster, and zone two is the first ring outside of the inner circle. For the more adventurous (or the more suburb loving), a person can also include higher numbered zones in a purchase of a tube pass, for a little bit more cash.

Our haphazard plans for the day would most likely include only Westminster and London. London, sometimes called "The City," is the financial center of the capital, and encompasses a square mile, which is only a tiny part of the entire metropolis. Westminster is a separate city to the west of London, and, like the entire area, takes on the name of London for simplicity's sake.

We purchased our tube passes and checked our watches. We realized it was a little too early to use our passes. For £3.90 a person can ride all day, but only after the peak hours, which end at 9:30. It was still early, so we decided to take a stroll towards Big Ben and the Houses of Parliament. Ben is the name of the sixteen-ton bell that's inside the clock tower at the Houses of Parliament, and is not the name of the bell tower itself. The bell was named for Sir Benjamin Hall, who was the Chief Commissioner of Works for Westminster when the bell was hung in 1858.

As we walked closer towards Big Ben, there were souvenir stands where it's possible to buy all kinds of nice things: postcards, books about London in various languages, life-size cardboard heads of Princess Di, and inflatable vinyl Big Ben Towers. I was tempted to buy a couple things: a Princess Di head and an inflatable Ben would be an interesting combination, and could possibly generate some amusement for me, but the day was early, and I had no intention of carrying around a bunch of souvenirs throughout the rest of the day.

I was surprised when I saw the real Big Ben tower close up. The tower is big all right, but not as lofty as I thought it might be. It does stand at 320 feet tall, which is good-sized, indeed. Maybe it's the tower's girth that takes the sense of proportion to another dimension. It is an impressive sight and much more interesting to look at compared to anything in my little town back home.

The tower's clocks read twenty past nine, and the time was growing near when our tube passes would be accepted, so went to the nearest tube stop, and through the turnstiles leading to the tube platform to board our underground train.

I'm impressed by those little machines that read commuters' tickets. The paper pass is put into a slot next to the turnstiles, the machine gobbles the tube ticket in a quick slurp, reads the pass, and then decides to either spit it out in a slot a few inches from where it was deposited, or, if the tube pass has expired, to keep it for further digestion. It's a marvel of technology, and seems to go unnoticed by everyone hurrying on to destinations important.

We had decided to go to an antiques market. Bill was eager to go to the market, and I wanted to get my bearings in London, and this seemed like a good way to go about that. To get to this market, we passed through the Angel underground station, one of the deepest undergrounds in London, from what Bill told me. Judging from the length and the slant of the escalator (almost straight up), I believed this to be true. This was almost like an odd prelude to an amusement park ride.

Emerging from a tube station and into the daylight, we found the antiques market and did some browsing; Bill looked at a few things and I did, too. The one thing that caught my eye was a toilet paper holder. Though I was positive it wasn't a genuine antique, I liked it, and figured it was worth the handwritten £4.00 price sticker. It's a nice little painted brass piece, with a wooden spool, and with large lettering across the face of it that reads: "TOILET" in bold, capital letters. I thought it would look great in the bathroom back home. A few minutes after making my purchase, I noticed the proprietor of the stand reach into a large corrugated box, and draw from it a near duplicate of what I had just purchased, and place it on the table in his booth. It's a good little souvenir, one that will be made useful on a daily basis, and well worth £4.00.

There was an interesting old map store that we spent a few minutes in, and we had a look around for a shop that Bill had visited on a previous trip to this London neighborhood. No matter how many times we went in and out of one old building, down the staircase and back around, the business he wanted to stop into seemed to have vanished. We hiked around the neighborhood some more, taking in several additional stores, all the while working up an appetite.

It was going on noon, and we found an admirable pub called The Agricultural, at 13 Liverpool Road. Outside, plants hung from wrought iron on either side of the front door, and globe-like lights offset the green paint and brass trim in a fashionable manner. Inside, the pub was clean, tidy, and waiting for the lunch crowd to arrive. Everything looked delicious on the lunch menu as we stood at the food-ordering counter. I decided on a ham sandwich, which included lettuce, tomato, and cucumber, with a glass of bitter (for the sole purpose of washing down my lunch). Bill ordered a ham and cheese on a crusty roll, and had a glass of bitter, also, with his lunch. A barkeep-in-training gained expert advice from the pub's manager on how to pour a draught so it foams in the glass just so. I watched diligently in case I should ever need this knowledge, although I was just a bit distracted by this young woman's grace and intensity of purpose.

Our bitters and food were great, the toilet facilities were more than adequate, and we moved on to an outdoor street market. These outdoor markets can be found all over the city, and seem to be a handy site to buy groceries, clothing, pet supplies, CDs, tapes, books, and plenty of other items of necessity. Neither of us really needed anything at the market, and we were inclined to move on to another area of town. We didn't necessarily have a plan for the afternoon, though. Bill made a suggestion that was top-notch. He asked if I'd want to try to find Abbey Road Studios, the place where that old band, The Beatles, used to record.

I was all for that. The Beatles have always been at or near the top of my favorite band list. When I was two years old I used to sit out on the swing in the back yard and warble "I Want to Hold Your Hand" over and over again, much to the amusement of our next door neighbor, Mrs. Finch, who would listen in on my impromptu concerts. A few years later, I would sit in a friend's bedroom after school and encourage him to play the *Abbey Road* album as many times as possible before it was time for me to go home for supper.

Then I started playing the guitar. After fumbling around with a couple cheap guitars that were monsters to play and which required intense pressing down on the strings, which didn't always lend itself to a golden tone (and the guttural resonance was not always my fault), I encountered a genuine 1960's Gretsch Tennessean. This was exactly the same model that the Beatles' guitarist, George Harrison, used to play. I had found precisely what I wanted, and I bought the Gretsch guitar. From that point on, I had to buy the biggest Beatles songbook that I could find, and learn the chords to all the songs that weren't too tricky to play.

A visit to Abbey Road Studios, as long as we were in London, seemed to be a very good idea.

Bill had a good, general idea of how to get to Abbey Road from some directions he had scribbled down off the Internet. We needed to take a tube to the St. John's Wood Underground Station, then find a main road, which would lead us to the studios after a couple short blocks' walk. Bill and I are both blessed with the uncanny aptitude of finding the exact wrong way to turn, whether in new surroundings or even old, familiar locales. After getting off the Underground at St. John's Wood, we blundered around the pavements for a good half-hour before we realized we weren't getting any closer to our chosen destination. In fact, we were walking around in a large, ungainly circle.

Thinking back to one of the James Herriot books that I had read, I remember that author mentioning he had spent some time at the Lord's Cricket Ground while in the Royal Air Force. With a twinge of enjoyment, I noted that we were right where he had written about; but it really wasn't where we wanted to be, even though it seemed a very nice neighborhood with well kept houses and tidy yards.

Our map gave us little guidance. The area that we were in was just out of the map's projection of where the model London tourist might investigate. As much and as intently as we stared at the map, the intersection at which we were standing was not on the map, and never would be. We backtracked, and with a little luck, we found a street that Bill had scribbled the name of on his notepaper. A few more minutes of walking, and we were at the famous zebra crosswalk that is pictured on the *Abbey Road* album cover.

A couple doors down from the crosswalk is a nondescript white building with a small lighted sign above the doorway that reads: "Abbey Road Studios." We had found it. There are a number of graffiti scribblings on the low, concrete wall that is in front of the studio offices. Not any of the graffiti is really worth noting, although someone, most likely a Pink Floyd fan or some other troublemaker, had spray painted "Dark Side of the Moon" across a large portion of the wall.

There was another American visiting this afternoon. It was a guy wearing sweat clothes and a Boston Red Sox jacket, taking picture after picture of the front of the building, and topping off his pilgrimage by adding his scrawl to the graffiti wall.

I've always liked the Beatles, but I was content with my visit to this shrine after snapping a couple pictures, and walking across the zebra crossing. Oh, I did have to pause for a couple minutes to sit on the bench next to the "Abbey Road NW8 City of Westminster" street sign to take the setting in, and I did purchase a couple items at the Abbey Road souvenir shop a block down the street: a postcard and a key ring.

Departing from the area, we found that Abbey Road Studios is only a couple blocks away from the St. John's Wood tube stop. Why it took us so long to walk in the correct direction in the first place, I'll never know. I wouldn't be surprised that the next time I'm in this neighborhood I'll zig when I should zag, and I'll be in the same lost state again.

We stopped into London's *official* Beatles store, but I couldn't find anything in there worth purchasing and then lugging around. After all, I already had my souvenir toilet paper holder, what more could a person require?

In the tube station, going back to the B&B, Bill was asked by a well-dressed African gent if he could have some money for a phone call, as this man had lost his money, passport, and other belongings. Bill gave him enough to get started on a phone call, though not more than that. There are a few rascals that hang out in any city, asking for money. Better to ask for it, I suppose, rather than outright taking a person's cash. This man seemed genuine in his appeal, and even if it was only an act, it was worth a pound, or whatever it was that Bill passed on to him, to hear this man's unfortunate tale.

In retrospect, it might have been a nice gesture on our part to lead this man to an attendant at the underground station, so he could gain proper assistance, and maybe even find his way to his country's embassy for further help. If he were genuine, we would have done him a favor, if he were a fake, it would have been great to have seen his reaction.

Without much remorse at not having done more for this gent, we boarded our tube to Victoria Station to make our way back the B&B for a late afternoon break from the day. We made a stop at a take-away in Victoria Station for a snack. I found a cheese and tomato croissant for £1.75, and Bill decided on a sweet roll from another nearby take-away.

At a green grocer close to the B&B, we picked up some soft drinks and Barbecue Beef Hula-Hoops. Hula-Hoops are small rings of thick potato chips, and are a good, crunchy accompaniment to a sandwich. We ate our snacks at the B&B. Mine was filling and tasty. Bill said his was good also; his roll was not overly sweet, which was nice for him, but the roll had dates in it, and dates are something he prefers not to eat.

In the evening, we had a nighttime look at Big Ben, and went inside Westminster Abbey. Westminster Abbey is renowned as the burial place of some of England's royalty, and has been the coronation site of most of England's Kings and Queens. Memorials to poets, writers and musicians (including Shakespeare, Handel, and Dickens) are in Poets' Corner. The church was built beginning in the 13th Century, and has held up well.

This must be a fine looking church indoors in the daylight, with the light streaming in through the stained glass windows. As it was, we were there after nightfall, and the entire scene inside looked maybe even more demure and decidingly quiet and spiritual. Walking through the abbey were only a few other tourists this evening, and all of us spoke in quiet, hushed tones.

Magnificent. It's an impressive old place.

After finishing our quiet self-guided tour, we paused to reflect on the day at the Black Friar, which is a happy old pub right outside the Black Friar tube stop.

Right outside the tube stop, that is, if a person walks in the correct direction once leaving that tube station. It took a few tries to find the pub, walking around this way and that way, but once we were there, we found it to be a warm, friendly establishment. It was built in 1875, though it seems older than that, and is on the site of what used to be a Dominican monastery. The Tetley's was smooth and creamy; the Adam's was good, but a little less smooth and creamy. Above our table, carved in stone, was Humpty Dumpty on a frieze, gently reminding us, "Wisdom is Rare."

After a couple pints in this smoky pub, we thought that we'd move on closer to our "home." Passing by a thin, shaky young man with hollowed out eyes, who asked for money in a tiny voice, we boarded our tube.

I had heard about the low-brows that can frequent the tubes after nightfall, and I am proud to say that after consuming a goodly amount of beers and ales I had perhaps become one of the ones that some try their best to avoid. I grabbed a seat next to a young, clean cut man, who was clutching a Polish-English dictionary. As I sat down and breathed out a sigh of beer and other rank fumes which I had accumulated throughout the course of the evening, my tube car neighbor's fingers curled around his dictionary a little tighter than previously, and he inched as far away from me as his seat would allow.

CHAPTER FOUR

A Double Decker Red Tour Bus and Evening Entertainment

Down the stairs to the basement breakfast room. How many steps did I count? I tried to put a number on each footfall as I headed down the staircase; I lost track. There were somewhere around 65 steps (give or take) to get to the breakfast room at the Georgian House. The same breakfast was offered as the previous morning: cereal, orange juice, canned peaches, canned grapefruit, toast (in a nice little toast cooling rack, which keeps the toast crisp), a runny egg, bacon, and mushrooms. I declined the possibility of sausages and tomato, though. There are little packets available of orange marmalade and of brown sauce. Brown sauce is a dark, runny liquid that tastes somewhat like American steak sauce. The bacon is interesting; it's more akin to Canadian bacon (or what might be called back bacon), than the rashers of bacon strips that are found in the States. As today I didn't order tomato or sausage with breakfast, I received double the mushrooms and double the bacon.

(These people at the bed and breakfasts really don't want to send any of their guests out feeling less than stuffed.)

It's a little slower going up the sixty-some steps after breakfast compared to going down the flights of stairs on an empty stomach. Bill waited for me downstairs in the lobby, as I had decided to brush my teeth and stuff a few essentials into my pockets after breakfast.

We had our room for only two nights, and the hotel was booked full after that. This was the morning we were to be kicked out of the Georgian House Hotel, and we began a hunt for a different B&B in the same area. We checked out a lot of places. Of the B&B's that had vacancies, either the available rooms were up on the top floors, or the place was a dump. If not exactly a dump, then the place left something to be desired. I'm surprised that they don't slap on a coat of paint or re-glue the wallpaper to the walls at some of these B&B's, but I suppose the owners figure why bother, as the rooms get rented out, regardless. We had no luck at the Arden, the Chevoit, the Ivy Inn, the Holly Inn, or at many other possible lodgings.

Eventually, we found a place close by, called the Jubilee. The reception area wasn't too bad, and the sample room that Bill trusted me to look at seemed OK. When we checked in, we found the room that was actually available was not very big at all, and very narrow; two tiny twin beds in what Bill called the smallest room that he's ever stayed in at a B&B in his many trips to England. There were three rolls of toilet paper in the loo, with two choices of color to decide upon once the suitable moment to grasp the roll of toilet paper arrived: lime green and tangerine orange. I've never encountered toilet paper in these lively shades, ever. The lamp cords by the bed pillows dangled around precariously, and only one of the lamps was functioning.

It was late morning by the time were back to our sightseeing. Today it was the *Original London Sightseeing Bus Tour* that would take us around London. Starting in the early morning, this would be a great way to spend an entire day, hopping off at the places that a person wants to see, then hopping back on at leisure. You pay one time up front for the ticket, then you can get off and on their busses as many times as you'd like during a twenty-four hour period. There are four tour routes that are offered, so you can really cover the city well. There are several bus companies that offer this same type of sightseeing tour, but we chose *The Original* because we happened to have a coupon for a few pounds off the regular price. The way I see it, if a pound is saved here and a pound is saved there, that'll pay for at least a couple pints at the end of the day.

Before boarding the tour bus, we were given small headsets, which could be plugged into a choice of several holes next to the bus seats. Each port promised a running commentary of the sights in various languages. I chose English, as that's the only language I have any hope of understanding. This recorded narration would have been enlightening, I'm sure, if the earphones would have stayed in place. Maybe it's the shape of my ears, but those darn things wouldn't stay in place. I wiggled them around in my ears, shoved both hands up against my ears, tried concentrating on just plugging one ear with the audio presentation, but still, the earphones kept falling out. I looked around. No one else was having this problem. I sighed, and resigned myself to the fact that I was a misfit on this double-decker tour bus, and got what I could out of the recorded presentation, which wasn't a whole lot.

We had boarded the bus across from Victoria Station, and we chose our seats on the upper deck, which seemed much more agreeable than being confined to the seats below. We then traveled through a section of London that included Hyde Park's Speakers' Corner (where anyone can talk about anything on any Sunday), and the Marble Arch, built in 1827 at a cost of £10,000. Originally, the Marble Arch was positioned as an entrance to Buckingham Palace; it was moved in 1851 to where it now stands, in the midst of a traffic island. We went up and down streets, rounding bends, and taking in the scenery. I occasionally heard expressions of exclamation from my fellow passengers, and I looked around to see eyebrows raised and looks of astonishment on faces. Obviously something rousing was being mentioned on the audio recording, but I was oblivious to it, although I was enjoying the ride.

Bill and I hopped off the bus at mid-day, at the Baker Street Station, where we found a cafeteria style restaurant, the aptly named Baker Street Food Station. I had their dish of the day: pasta with tomato, zucchini, onion, potato, and tomato sauce. Bill had a pasta dish also. We walked off a little bit of the meal, bought some mints and other candies at a newsstand, then boarded an *Original* bus waiting for customers. It was the upper deck again, and another prerecorded tour.

There was a little time before this driver began his section of the tour, so I figured this would be a good time to really get a handle on getting those earphones jammed into my ears. That never happened; I still had problems trying to keep those little plugs stuck in place.

Once we noticed that the weather was changing somewhat, we had scooted toward the front of the upper deck. It was a little colder than when we had started out on our tour, and the enclosed windbreak provided some relief once the bus driver fired his vehicle up and we set out on the next section of this jaunt. We were still on the upper level, but somewhat out of the cool November air, and we still had a great vantage point to look out on the city.

We went down Marylebone Road, Portland Place, and Regent Street, past Piccadilly Circus, and Trafalgar Square. When the driver stopped at Whitehall, we hopped off to try our luck at finding play tickets for the evening in Leicester Square.

A month or two before we took our journey, Bill and I had e-mailed each other frequently about what we'd like to do on the trip. We had gone in fits and starts for a while, sometimes finding common ground, other times not. Bill had mentioned that maybe we should take in a play while in London. I had the opposite opinion, though Bill said that he'd been to a play or two in London before and it was worth the while. I had been to a just a few plays in my life, and I was thinking that I really wasn't that interested in taking in the London theater scene. I was of the opinion that after a hard day of sightseeing, I would prefer to spend a bit of time relaxing in a pub, sampling English ales, rather than sit in some stuffy playhouse watching actors recite memorized lines.

When Bill told me that *Mamma Mia!* has been an ongoing play in London, and that it features the music of Abba, as well having performed to sold-out crowds for some time, I slowly began to gain interest in seeing a play in London. I had joined a record club when I was a pre-teen, and Abba's *Arrival* album was one of the records that I had bought on my first purchase from the club. Abba was a fine old band, and when I learned that a couple members of Abba had played a large part in the score of the play, I was ready to go.

Now, we were walking around in Leicester Square, London's home of theater tickets, and in search of tickets for *Mamma Mia!*

We had hoped to purchase a pair of discount tickets at the famous Half Price Ticket Booth, but, after walking around Leicester Square for awhile, and being accosted by youths attempting to give us free bags of microwave popcorn (some sort of promotion, I believe, or maybe they were just being generous), we couldn't find the famed booth. We decided to inquire at The Leicester Square Box Office Half Price Discount Theatre Tickets storefront for their offerings of play tickets for the evening. This was, after all, an official agent, according to their sign. *Mamma Mia!* was selling at over forty pounds per seat, but, supposedly, they were good seats. Good seats or not, that was around sixty U.S. dollars and too costly for what was in my wallet.

Poking around the various ticket agencies, we thought about an alternative to *Mamma Mia!*, but decided that this was the play we were going to see, by gosh, and we could find some less expensive seats elsewhere. We chose Half Price and Discount Theatre Tickets, which also seemed a reputable place of business, and we discovered that they offered dress circle seats for a price more within our budgets. Dress circle, we were to find out, was the third balcony, but we were to be in the front row of that section, which seemed as if it would be admirable for the ticket price of £25.00 each.

Once we had gotten our vouchers for the tickets, we set out to find the playhouse, The Prince Edward Theatre, for a two-fold purpose. One, to make sure that we could actually find the Prince Edward later in the day, once it was dark; two, to verify that we could, indeed, turn these vouchers into actual tickets. If there was the small chance that the vouchers were not really for the play, we'd rather know that in the middle of the afternoon, rather than just before show time.

Any slight qualm that either of us had experienced was quickly laid to rest, as we found the theater without too much of a problem (although it was undergoing a facelift, and was slightly obscured by scaffolding). The Prince Edward was just a bit off Charing Cross Road, and in a handy Soho location. Inside, to cash in our vouchers for actual tickets, we realized we could have just walked up to the box office, and purchased the same or nearly identical seats, and saved the pound surcharge that the ticket agency placed on its price. We had our tickets, anyway, and we strolled around Soho for awhile to take in the neighborhood.

Bill made a stop at a red phone box to call his wife back home in the states, to let her know that we were still on the face of this Earth, and to check on her and their kids' well-being. I waited a few feet away from the phone box, and gained many curious glances from passersby as I stood, propped up against the wall. Some marched bravely on, after making slight eye contact; others shied away, as much as the sidewalk would allow. Looking over towards the phone box, and wondering how much longer Bill would be on the phone, I caught that Bill was carefully prying a few little postcard sized souvenir advertisements off the walls of the phone box.

As he hung up the phone and opened the door, Bill had wide eyes, raised eyebrows, and a devious grin. Clutched in his hand were advertisements for: *Japanese Beauty, Petite Young Oriental, Autumn Megga Boobs, Natalie ("Genuine Photo"),* and *Voluptious Black Model.* The latter had the official name of *Boob Bondage Inc.* She was pictured with nearly half a beach nearly covering her ample bosom, and *Voluptuous* was misspelled. "I think her name might be 'Sandy,'" Bill offered, as he handed the souvenirs to me.

As we walked back to the bus stop, we saw the actual Half Price Ticket Booth, not in the rush of Leicester Square, but in a kiosk off to the side.

Finishing up the afternoon, we took the rest of the tour bus loop through London. This bus had an actual person for its guide, which was refreshing after I had wrestled with my earplugs earlier in the day. The bus took us through the City of London: down Fleet Street, past St. Paul's Cathedral, the Tower of London, supposedly past the Globe Theatre (though we stretched our necks and couldn't pick out the Globe), and the tremendously large London Eye, which, at 443 feet high, is the largest observation wheel on the planet. At this point it was getting just a little too cold on the upper level of the bus, and we moved downstairs.

It was crowded on the lower berth, and we sat next to some fellow Americans, Texans, who had a comment about everything, and who quizzed the tour guide on where to get some "real food" in London.

The bus snaked its way back to the Victoria Station stop, where we got off to walk back to the B&B to get ready for our night at the playhouse.

Going back to Soho for the play was a quick tube ride away. The Charing Cross stop is where we got off and made our way past the street's bookshops and nudged our way through the spirited evening crowd. There was still time for supper and we found a place called the Musicians' Café, off the main street. The restaurant was less than fifty feet from Charing Cross Road, but out of all the hustle and bustle. Good for us, bad for business at the café, it seemed, at least at the hour we were there. We both ordered Italian beers, I had a chicken sandwich and chips (a.k.a. French fries), and Bill ordered a dish with a fancy Italian name, which was rich with linguini, much to his dismay, as he had had plenty of pasta for lunch. His dinner was served with an olive oil herb sauce, bits of Italian sausage, and grated Parmesan cheese. The Musicians' Café was a great place, with friendly service and old guitars on the walls. After paying our bill and walking out the door, we didn't make it too far before Bill thought that he might go back to the café to pick up his umbrella, which was propped up near the seat he had occupied. We made it to the theater with five minutes to spare before the curtain lifted.

It was a good play – Björn Ulvaeus and Benny Andersson from Abba did the musical score; there were a few jokes that I couldn't figure out (one joke about an area of London called Chelsea was *huge*); the gent sitting to my right had a great chuckle going throughout almost the entire performance. The seats were good; we were up on dress circle balcony, but, as promised, in the front row of that section.

The songs were certainly catchy. Lots of audience participation, with clapping along to the beat in all the irresistible places. (Anyone ready for a round of "Chiquitita"?) Half ways though the play, at the interval, we had some ice cream. After the show, I couldn't help but notice all the yellow bicycle taxis driving people around; we stopped into the Three Greyhounds for a half-pint of Tetley's before it got too crowded in there. Then it was back to the tube to make our way to our Victoria Station stop. It was going on 11:00 PM by the time we got back to the B&B area. Just enough time to stop in at the friendly Country Pub, down the street from the Georgian House, for a pint of Guinness and a few peanuts before time was called for the evening.

CHAPTER FIVE

West to Wales

I was fine with a smaller breakfast in the morning. Cereal only, I thought, although the full English breakfast was offered to me. After mulling the situation over, I decided to take the Jubilee up on toast and bacon with my corn flakes. The toast was fine (it's hard to make bad toast, although most people have at one time or another, I know I have); the bacon was something that the kitchen help tossed into the microwave for a minute to warm it up. I was having this breakfast solo, as Bill had gotten up early to go to the Bermondsey Antiques Market. I was on my own for the morning, and I decided to take in a portion of the Victoria neighborhood after breakfast.

Poking my head out the window, I realized that this was the first day of the Britain visit where I would need my sunglasses. The sky was bright and clear. Now…where were those sunglasses? An exhaustive search in the bedroom led me right to them (underneath my suitcase, exactly where I had left them, for some unknown reason; and the glasses were barely bent).

Out in the crisp morning air, the first thing I had planned on doing was to find the Internet café that I had noted upon arriving into Victoria the first night. Actually, this was the only plan I had for the morning, but at least I was not without a mission. I thought it might be nice to write to the States about the visit so far. Up and down the street I went, and the Internet café was not to be found. Strange, I was sure that I had seen it a few nights ago. Could it have closed up in the meantime? I doubted that. I figured it was most likely either right underneath my nose, or a half block away, in a direction that I didn't search in.

My search had taken on the tones of a fruitless mission, and I had had enough looking for the Internet place. I wasn't desperate enough to ask for directions. I turned down a side street, and found a street market just setting up for the day's business. There were fresh fruits, fresh vegetables, fresh baked goods, and fresh fish. I bought grapes (at a pound for 80p), and bananas at an equally reasonable price; a lady was selling red plastic poppies, for Remembrance Day, and I thought I would donate a few coins and wear a poppy on my jacket. I went back to the B&B to meet up with Bill for the 10:30 AM checkout time.

A month before this trip began, we had purchased Britrail *Weekender* passes, which are valid for unlimited train travel over the course of four days, as long as the travel days include a Saturday and a Sunday and the travel takes place in the off-season. We had decided to go all out, and buy the first class passes rather than the standard class passes, as the price difference was minimal for these four-day vouchers. Not all the trains have first class cars, some lines have only standard class, but the Britrail Weekender first class pass was $130.00, compared to a standard class pass at $103.00. I'll take my chances and hope for trains with the first class cars. It seems as if most of the major routes have first class service.

This was Friday, and it was the day that we had anticipated heading north to the city of York to begin our first class rail journeys.

While Bill was out, he had the foresight to check on the rail service schedules for the northbound trains to Yorkshire. There had been heavy rains over the previous couple weeks, which had left some sections of the rails impossible to travel on. Our plans to immediately head to York were put on hold, as we discovered that this was a section of the rail system that was out of commission.

It was a little past the Jubilee's 10:30 checkout time as we sat in our room, contemplating a Britrail map. We couldn't stay at the B&B much longer while coming up with an alternate plan, and, with an amount of haste, we decided that west to Wales would be a good choice. Swansea was at the end of one particular line. With our rail passes, we could either ride to the end of the line, or get off whenever we pleased, and catch another train at our leisure.

We settled our bill, and headed out the door.

After toting our bags down to the Victoria Station, and getting on a tube to make our rail connection westbound at the Paddington Station, we were more than anxious to find out how to use our Britrail passes.

A ticket counter seemed like a good place to start.

We stood in the queue for a short bit, then talked to a greasy-haired youth manning a ticket window, who said that he couldn't help us, but that if we were to go to the first class ticket agents, one of them could validate our passes. The first class ticket agents were across the way, and we went to that section of the station. A very kind woman said that she didn't have to do anything with our passes. All we had to do was to get on a train, and the conductor would validate them. However, as long as we were there looking needy and confused, she stamped both our passes anyway. It felt as if we had gotten something important accomplished. We were now official.

On the train, we realized that first class is the way to go with these Britrail passes. The seats on a Great Western first class car are good and wide (they're probably built that way to handle the excess of all the nourishing English breakfasts), copies of the *Daily Telegraph* newspaper are set out at each table, an attendant pushes a refreshment trolley through the cars with complimentary tea, coffee, and biscuits.

Sandwiches and hot food can be purchased, such as mature cheese ploughman's sandwiches, prawn and mayonnaise sandwiches, and Patak's chicken tikka masala and rice. You can buy some Brannigan's Beef and Mustard Crisps to go with your sandwich, and wash the lot down with a John Smith's Smooth Bitter or a glass of Beau Mayne Chateau Bottled Red Bordeaux. And for dessert, if you are up for it: a luxury cake slice.

An announcement came over the speakers on the train: "Should our customers require baguettes, please come to car F, the buffet car, in the center of the train." "Buffet" was pronounced *buffy*, as it should be, rather than *buff-ay*. Myself, I didn't require any baguettes, just some tea, some coffee at one point, and a plastic wrapped pack of shortbread biscuits.

I'd say that the most interesting experience I've had using a toilet in quite some time came on that Great Western train to Wales. I'd never been on a train for this long before, and after a couple hot caffeine-laden beverages, I was eager to discover where the train's loo was kept, and what is was like.

Looking behind me, I saw the lighted sign: "Toilet." Ahhh…good. I stood as the train bumped and shifted along. Stumbling around like a drunken sailor in the gangway, I came to the automatic door: *Whoosh!* It opened to let me into the link between cars where the toilet is kept. A brief stumble, then I opened up the toilet door. Stumbling and swaying again, I grabbed the handgrip in the compartment to steady myself. After I did my business, I was wondering how to flush the toilet. The lever, it turned out, looked just like a handgrip, only a little smaller. Deciding that it was ok to flush the toilet as were not stopped at a train station (the waste goes out directly onto the train tracks, I believe), I flushed, then turned towards the sink. There's a little rubber ball on the floor that can be stepped on for hand-washing water. If it is stepped on with enough vigor, more than a dribble comes out of the faucet. A knob is available to adjust the water temperature; there is a nondescript smelling soap, and roll of clean, striped towels.

CHAPTER SIX

Rain and Brains in Cardiff

The train proceeded west, past Slough, Reading, Didcot, a fine looking nuclear energy power plant, Swindon, and Bristol Parkway. At Bristol Parkway, it was announced that we were ahead of schedule, and we would wait at the station for ten minutes until we were back on schedule. Shortly afterwards, we passed across a bridge which would take us into Wales.

With eager expectations, both Bill and I looked out our windows as we were about to make our first encounter with this foreign country; once we reached Newport, we knew for sure that we were in Wales. Almost solely because of our map, though. The scenery looked very similar to the scenery that we had just enjoyed in England, although there was a sign announcing that we were not passing merely through Newport, but the sign also had Newport's Welsh name of *Casnewydd* on it. Somewhere in the back of my mind, I had expected that immediately upon arriving in Wales I would see a mountainous landscape filled with Welsh farmers, Welsh sheep, and Welsh slate mining remains. The scenery was nice, though, and the Welsh language on the sign reminded me that I was a little closer, logistically, towards my home in the U.S., but somehow more distant. I found myself liking this journey more and more all the time.

As we passed from Newport and rode nearer to Cardiff, Bill and I dug out our Britrail map. We had been considering going to the end of this rail line, to Swansea, but now were having other thoughts. Night would be falling soon, and a light rain was beginning to come down.

The connections pictured on the map from Swansea up to Yorkshire looked like they would take us through many small towns in Wales (which would be a nice way to travel on the trains, if we had a little extra time), but all those stops might take up too much of the following day. Or, we could double back after visiting Swansea and take extra time backtracking our rail route to get to Yorkshire. It was announced that we were about to arrive at the Cardiff rail station. With only slight hesitation, and barely folding our map, we grabbed our suitcases, and jumped off the train to set foot in Cardiff. It was the best fit of spontaneity to come along for either of us in some time.

Once off the train, we looked around for signs pointing us to the Tourist Information office. The map that we had with us looked as if it was pinpointing the Tourist Information office for Cardiff right at the train station, but we didn't see any of those helpful little blue *TI* logos in any direction that we turned in.

I've read that a friendly bobby is a good person to ask if one is looking for a place that is not where a person hoped it would be. And, luck! A quartet of bobbies was just up the way from us. Unfortunately for us, they were visitors in town also (from Brighton), and didn't know about the TI in Cardiff. They did point out, though, that we were at the Cardiff Central rail station, the main rail station in Cardiff, and that was exactly where we needed to be in order to be closest to city centre, and the TI couldn't be far away. With a thank you, and a look around to see if we could find a local who could direct us, we approached some rail station employees who inquired if we had train tickets. We said we did, and they, in return, gave us directions for a short walk to what amounted to going across the street, and there we were, right where we wanted to be, at the Tourist Information office.

We poked around the TI for a few minutes, picking up some brochures about Cardiff, then walked up to the counter to inquire about booking a B&B for the night. Some might frown on the idea of paying a slight upcharge for the convenience of booking a room with the TI's assistance. The TI will charge a slight commission, and they also garner a part of the B&B' owners' take on letting the room, but if a person is in a town that he's not familiar with, the TI's guidance is worth a pound or two. As I see it, the B&B is using the TI to rent a room that may have otherwise gone unused for the evening, so everyone's satisfied: the Tourist Information office gets a little commission, the bed and breakfast receives rent on a room, and the wayfaring tourist doesn't have to knock on doors in inclement weather to hopefully try to land a decent place to lay his head for the night.

The young women at the TI's counter asked us to fill out a short questionnaire about what we were looking for in a B&B. We were open to something simple: two beds, a bathroom, a place close to city centre, as well as close to the rail station, and all at a reasonable price. After carefully tabulating our answers, the young women directed us to The Big Sleep. A singular name for a modest bed and breakfast, we both agreed, but we were trusting in these kind souls to lead us to what they thought would accommodate our needs to the best of their abilities. They gave us a map, taking the time to highlight our walking route to The Big Sleep, and sent us on our way.

We walked through Cardiff's rain, studied our map, and were surprised when we saw a multi-story hotel up the road from us, with the sign outside reading: The Big Sleep. We found the reception desk (which was not immediately inside the front door, but up on the second floor), checked in, and were pleased to find that two travelers on a budget could take a first class train ride during the day, and then check in to a decent hotel in the evening. Bed and Breakfast inns can be enjoyable, but a hotel room was more than we expected for the price that we paid.

The Big Sleep used to be an office building, and was built in the 1960's rendering of what modern should look like. After ending its career as an office building, it was vacant for several years, but took on a new life as this hotel about a year before our visit. Everything looked pretty well fresh and newly done. The paint on the hallway walls is purple; the carpeting throughout the halls is a darker shade of purple, with decorative yellow *Z's*, zigzagging every direction in which we turned.

This hotel has almost everything a person could ask for in a lodging: hot and cold running water that arrive out of the same tap (although I never did become proficient at operating the buttons on the water knobs that control the pressure and temperature), a heated towel rack, a heater for the room, big windows (with views of an ice rink down the street, a toy store, various city buildings, and the top of a domed stadium in the heart of the city), there were individual lights for each bed, and duvets on the beds. The electric supply was mystifying, though. Like other places, it took some doing to figure out which switch to flip first to make another switch work. The white motif of the room, with light-colored wood, was a welcome contrast to the purple hallways.

We had a good look around the city, walking down Bute Terrace to the ice rink, turning right to Hayes Bridge Road, St. John's Street, Duke Street, looping around to High Street, St. Mary Street, Custom House Street, and back to Bute Terrace, then setting out again, but taking a slightly different route. There were several entrepreneurs selling pennants, caps, scarves, and other souvenirs at various stands along the sidewalk. Many offered to exchange their goods for our money, but, sadly for the merchants, not one sale was made to either myself or to Bill.

Cardiff is an engaging city by dusk and night in a light rain. It would be interesting to take it in on a warm, clear spring day. There are several Victorian-style shopping arcades, which sell everything one could ask for. One of the arcades that we visited, the Cardiff Central Market, has a huge upper floor devoted to two shops: a record/tape/CD shop, and a pet shop. You can look down from the upper floor to the ground level and take it all in, in a pseudo-Victorian manner. A live flop-eared bunny can be purchased upstairs for a pet, and you can stroll downstairs to buy a full, skinned bunny for supper at one of the arcade's butcher shops.

After coming across the monumental Cardiff Castle (too dark, too rainy, and too late in the day to tour it), and seeing a sign with the tongue twister of a name, *Llanfairpwllgwyngyllgogerychwyrndrobwllll-lantysiliogogogoch* (that's "The Church of Mary In the Hollow of the White Hazel Near the Fierce Whirlpool and the Church of Tysilio by the Red Cave" to you and to me), we stopped into a pub called The Goat's Major to test the city's local brew, Brains. I tried a Brains Dark, which was good, and tasted true to its name; Bill tried a Brains also, and was suitably satisfied, as well.

We walked past the recently constructed and aptly named Millenium Dome, and saw that there was some sort of affair about to take place, possibly a sporting event of some type. We now realized that the ped-dlers, whom we kept encountering on the street, were attempting to make a profit off the evening's entertainment at the Millenium Dome.

We made a couple more stops, including one at an Internet café, called the Internet Exchange. After filling out their forms to be enlisted into a free membership at the Internet Exchange, and earn loyalty points for each visit, we set down at computers to send off a few emails, and do a little surfing. Paying for the time spent on their computers on the way out (which was a reasonable price, around £1.00, give or take a few pence), I of course, forgot to give the clerk behind the counter my points score card so he could record my visit and stamp the card for val-idation. I like these sorts of cards that give me something free after spending so much money, or making so many purchases. The trouble is, I usually forget to use them.

We walked around the streets a little more, and were close enough to the train station to hopefully make use of their toilets to drain the beers out of our systems. From what we could tell, as Cardiff's nightlife began to pick up, it seemed to be ok to urinate against businesses' outside walls, and even defecate in parking lots, but we thought we'd take the more modest route, and use a facility with flushing capabilities. The rail station seemed an excellent choice.

Bill and I made it at least twenty yards into the rail station before being stopped by a security guard, inquiring if we had tickets to travel on the train that evening. Bill explained that no, we weren't traveling that night, but we just got into town earlier in the day, and we had walked into the train station again.

Gazing at us though his glasses with skeptical eyes, the guard asked why we were in the rail station, if we weren't traveling anywhere. Uh-oh! We were caught; Bill took the initiative to confess, "We're looking for the toilets."

The security guard was satisfied that we weren't troublemakers. In fact, we seemed to hit it off fairly well, once he recognized that we had American accents. A friendly smile beamed out from the guard's grey beard, and he asked about our trip, and told us that this was a big rugby weekend. Tonight, the match was Wales against New Zealand, and was expected to bring in an additional 10,000 people to the city. Saturday's match, the following night, was Wales vs. Samoa (or maybe it was Italy, I'm a little hazy on that detail), and an extra 60,000 to 70,000 people would be in Cardiff. There was extra security in the rail station in case the fans started to get out of line. That would explain the bobbies from Brighton that we saw when we first arrived.

It was fascinating, and we could have chatted all evening, but the time was drawing nearer to inquire as to how we could locate the nearest toilet facilities. With a set of directions that was far too complicated to master, we set out in the general direction the guard pointed to, up some stairs, down a corridor, down some stairs, all around. We couldn't find the facilities, and decided to just go back to the hotel instead. To leave the rail station, we had to walk past our guard again, and we hoped he wouldn't ask why we didn't walk in the direction of the toilets; we just wanted to leave the building. We scurried past, with a "thanks," a nod, and smiles exchanged amongst all concerned.

Bill and I were under agreement that it was drawing near to the time to find a place to eat, hopefully an establishment that was fairly noise-free, but yet served beer with their meals, and, of course, had toilets available for use.

We discovered that a thing to keep in mind for a visit to Cardiff is to eat early. The rule, we found out, and as I understand it, seems to be that in the tourist season the restaurants stop serving food at 7 PM, and in the off-season the restaurants close up for the night by 6 PM. Here it was, a little after 7 o'clock, and we did a lot of looking around, but found no place to get a substantial meal. (Although later on, I did notice advertisements in some city brochures for restaurants that do stay open late. Unfortunately, we didn't look at the brochures earlier.)

Thinking that the hotel surely must have a restaurant, we walked back to the Big Sleep as the rain grew heavier. No, no hotel restaurant. As I mentioned, The Big Sleep has *almost* everything a tourist could need. But we did each make a long-awaited trip to our room's bathroom.

We ventured back out into the rain. Poking our heads into a restaurant next door to the hotel, which had slipped beyond our notice previously, we inquired about their evening meal service. The restaurant was about to close up for the night, we were told. A family was putting on their coats as they were about to stroll out the door, being the last customers of the evening.

After some backtracking though the city, we wound up at an alley-like street that hosts a string of almost identical take-aways. The façades are slightly different, but the menus are about alike in these dozen or so take-aways. After considering a Donner sandwich—a spiced leg of meat (lamb is what most believe it to be), like what I'm accustomed to seeing in a Greek restaurant, is awaiting slicing. I decided on a Welsh pasty and chips with a Fanta to drink. Bill ordered a curry chicken with chips, and we went back to the hotel to watch a little rugby on the television. The commentary was in Welsh, which was fine, as we couldn't figure out the game anyway. Bill grumbled about the quality of his chicken curry; my pasty was greasy, but good. The thick, crusty lip on a pasty was excellent for the Welsh miners, who could take a pasty with them to the mines for lunch, grab the thick crust with their dirty hands, and throw away the soiled remains of the crust once the main part of the pasty was eaten. We each had enough chips with our entrées to keep a crew of miners fed for a week.

After supper, I was tired and ready for sleep, but Bill was alert and intent on watching television, reading, and also doing his nightly showering up to get fresh and ready for the following day's adventures. While Bill was in the shower, I flipped the lights off, and tried to doze, watching cartoons on the television to put my mind into no-man's land. The cartoons were the quality black and white kind, relaxing, and sent me into a light slumber, until Bill walked out of the bathroom, found the lights off, and stumbled around a little while attempting to negotiate his way around the room. Of course, he turned his bed light on and off, flipped around the television channels, rustled reading materials, sighed, and so on until the wee hours.

We're on slightly different sleep schedules, Bill and I. I tend to get really sleepy by around nine at night, and typically can't say awake past ten o'clock in any sort of logical frame of mind without some sort of stimulation. Bill, on the other hand, will stay up half the night, puttering around to his heart's content. I'm sure that my waking up early and brewing coffee and tea in the early morning hours is as confounding to him as his staying up late is to me.

CHAPTER SEVEN

A Nice English Rain

Bill slept in, while I took advantage of our luxurious bathroom facilities to get ready for the day. This morning, we would spend a few more hours in Cardiff, then travel on to the city of York; I took the elevator downstairs to the Big Sleep's auditorium-like breakfast room. It was a serve-yourself buffet, and I got there early enough to have the entire room almost to myself. There was bread, lightly singed croissants, lightly singed rolls, breakfast cereal (Special K, Corn Flakes, Weetabix, All-Bran, and many other choices), yogurt (I had strawberry), apples, orange juice, coffee, and tea. I didn't realize that the bread could be turned into make-your-own-toast until after I had buttered a couple slices. I had guessed that maybe regular ol' bread was a Welsh tradition for breakfast, until I saw the toasters. As I filled up my plate, thinking about how exciting it was to be in Cardiff, having a more than ample Welsh breakfast in the local tradition, one of the hotel's kitchen people came along, carrying additional offerings to the buffet.

She commented to me about the morning's weather, "A nice English rain."

Now I was slightly confused. I was sure I was in Wales, but why didn't she call this a Welsh rain? Maybe I'll never know, as I didn't ask. I should have inquired further.

The morning paper was available, and I had a quick read of it as I enjoyed this good and filling breakfast (going back for seconds on my favorites).

I had the duty of heading down to the train station after breakfast to find out what the best connection would be to Yorkshire on this rainy Saturday morning. Cardiff to Birmingham to Leeds, was what the information agent suggested, although the rail lines past Leeds may still be closed. In a fit of helpfulness, and for reasons that I didn't understand at all, the clerk talked on about how we would be better off going through Manchester to Leeds, and citing all the reason why this route was better than the one previously suggested.

"Whatever will get us there," I murmured to myself.

This woman was adamant about printing out her proposed schedule for me, which I was quite agreeable to have her do. I can listen to directions very well, comprehend them in an amazing fashion as they are being told to me, and recite them back verbatim. Two seconds after walking away, though, I forget the conversation completely. I really prefer to have written evidence of what I'm supposed to remember. She had quite a time trying to get her computer printer to spit out the information for me. After some cursing and then gaining assistance from a co-worker, she printed the train schedule out on another printer, apologized, and we parted ways.

On the way out of the train station I picked up a couple postcards and a Foster's Luxury Flapjack to eat later. A flapjack is a large, crumbly bar-type cookie: compressed oats and margarine with a chocolate flavored coating, 110 grams for 65 pence. Very good, but they make a mess on a train if you just nibble away at it, as I would find out. Like the pasty from the previous night, this is good, sturdy Welsh food.

Walking back to the hotel, the light rain turned into a downpour, and then some. This wasn't anything like the Midwestern rain that I'm used to, where a heavy rain comes down fiercely and usually straight down; this was a fine sprinkle which had gone mad and out of control, with a sideways blowing wind which whipped at me from every direction. In walking just a few blocks from the train station back to the Big Sleep, I got drenched. I had to have a complete change of clothing once I got back to the hotel, and then, regrettably, I stuffed the wet clothes into a plastic bag, and then the plastic bag into my suitcase. I was about to grow some mold on the clothing, it seemed, and there was nothing that could be done about it for the time being, as we were only a short time away from our train's departure, which would to take us to Yorkshire.

At quarter to eleven, Saturday morning, we were on the train out of Cardiff, leaving the rail station, and doing a little bit of backtracking, to Newport, where the train would then follow the rail line north, through Cwmbran, Pontypool and New Inn. About this time, there began an announcement that we were to hear time and time again: "We are very sorry for the delays." This was mentioned over the train's loudspeakers at least once every ten minutes. It was nice to know that the operators of the train are aware of their schedule, even if they're not able to stick to it.

The scenery was fantastic and delicious as we headed north: sharply rising hills, green grass, fertile farmlands, grazing sheep, and, once the sun made an appearance near Abergavenny, there was the largest rainbow that I've ever laid eyes on. The rainbow was only partially blotted out by the mud-streaked windows of the train. Past Llanvihangel Crucorney and Pandy, we entered western England, and rode through Pontrilas, Wormbridge, and Hereford.

All was uneventful. The announcements regarding the lateness of the train were regular, the group in front of my seat ordered a couple rounds of Stella Artois beer in tins, along with a cola for the youngster traveling with them, I munched on my luxury flapjack, scattering a few crumbs here and there, and thought that Shewsbury might be an interesting place to visit some day. The train took us past Shrewbury at a pretty good clip, but I did notice a big church with stained glass windows as well as a castle in that town. That's better, I suppose, than noting the town dump and the local power plant right away, although these things, too, have their merits.

More apologies. As we were now running an hour late, there would be complimentary coffee and tea served. The rail line was taking us past some large, pleasant hills, and a cup of tea sounded like a lovely way to accompany the scenery and enjoy the ride. When the trolley came around, I asked for my Ty-Phoo brand tea, plain, but it looked sort of off. Maybe there was just a smattering of milk that had gotten mixed in the cup, but it looked more than a little unappetizing, and the server didn't look like he was going to be too receptive to pouring another cup, so I dumped my complimentary tea in the trash. I had a plastic cup of Ty-Phoo earlier in the journey, and though that first one cost £1.10, at least that one was drinkable.

Looking for a little distraction, I decided to take a trip to the train car's toilet. This was fairly uneventful, except for tripping on some loose trim on the toilet's door, and attempting to get back into my car afterwards. The doors were automatic leading into the section with the toilet, but there was some art to getting back to my seat. I tried prying the glass doors apart with my hands. That didn't work, and I noticed a sign warning, "Do not touch glass." Above this warning sign, I noticed, there was a little button that read "Open." Feeling like a character in a Lewis Carroll book, I pushed the button. The door opened, and I stumbled back to my seat to leave my rear end in place until Manchester.

Or so I thought.

As the train was running so late, this train was going to terminate its route in Stockport, just outside of Manchester. We would need to disembark from the train, and wait for the next train to take us to Manchester to transfer again.

We waited on Stockport's Platform 4 amid the blue, orange and grey buildings for the Manchester train. It was only a few more minutes to Manchester once this train arrived. We spent a half-hour at the train station at Manchester, and spent a twenty pence coin each to use their facilities to pee and wash up. In the rail station's lavatory, there was a gent who hurdled the turnstile to get in. Either he was extremely eager to visit the toilets, or he was more of a cheapskate than I am. Up the staircase and to the platform, we waited in the diesel scented air for the train, where we found a first class car that would wind up taking us from Manchester to the next section of our day's journey.

I found a seat in this mostly empty car on the right side of the car, and Bill chose his seat across the aisle from me, on the left side of the car. The seats were red, speckled with grey, there were royal blue curtains on the windows, and little lamps gracing the tables. Quite nice.

The time was ten to four in the afternoon when we departed the station; shortly afterwards, the conductor came along to check for tickets. Bill showed him his Britrail pass, which satisfied the conductor. I drew out my pass, but the conductor just looked at the outside of my pass and nodded that I was fine for the trip. He didn't care to see the actual pass or look at the travel dates that it was good for. Maybe he noticed a family resemblance between Bill and myself, or possibly he thought I just looked like the type of man who would travel by no means other than first class. Whichever it was, it was enjoyable not to have a conductor scrutinize my railpass.

A man pushing a refreshment trolley arrived.

"Wonderful," I thought, "first class and another cup of free tea." Bill ordered a small bottle of red wine and paid for it. I asked the man for a cup of tea.

Eyeing me keenly and squarely, and with a look about him like a youngish Michael Palin wearing a silly rail attendant's uniform, he asked, "Do you have a first class ticket?"

My initial thought was *Hmmmmmm, wasn't that the conductor's job? And doesn't this young fellow look a bit like one of the comedians in that old Monty Python's Flying Circus television show?* But, I nodded the affirmative, said, "Yes," and began to pull out my first class rail pass.

"Well, why don't you have a drink card?"

Bill looked over from his seat across the way, and had a perplexed look on his face.

"Are you *sure* you have a first class ticket?"

"I have a rail pass."

"Oh, then you won't have a drink card."

The man, whom I decided (for lack of a better reference point) to refer to by the name of *Palin*, poured my tea, and asked for 85 pence. As I began to take out my wallet, I remembered that I had a jean pocket full of change, so I fished around in my pants for the change, and pulled out much less than 85p. Palin stood there, politely exasperated, doing his best not to make any eye contact whatsoever while I dug deeper to pull out a one pound coin. He got that, and I got my 15p change and my cup of tea. I supposed, later on, that if a person buys a train ticket at the rail station, a drink card is given for a tea or other light beverage, but with a railpass that step is removed, and there is no complimentary beverage. I should have reached out my leg and tripped Palin, though, for good measure, on his next walk through the car.

After all this, it was only just past four o'clock, the sun was falling lower in the sky, and the available light outside was growing dim. The green hillsides of England looked peaceful and relaxing in the dusk, then we entered a long tunnel, which blocked out the view. I dug the remains of my luxury flapjack out of my jacket pocket, sorted through the crumbs, spilling a few onto the floor, and wondered why there were police officers wandering around on this train.

We changed trains again in Leeds to go to York (the rail lines toward York were functioning despite the flooding in York). As we waited on the platform in Leeds, I felt a cold gaze reaching out from behind me. I turned around. It was Palin, again, still with his refreshment trolley. My God, he was stalking me. I met his eyes, and gave him a thin lift upwards of my lips and nodded. He turned quickly away, and so did I. Somehow, Palin and I had become enemies. I was guessing that he was going to be on this same train, serving refreshments in our car again. If he was in our car, I never saw him, as I was snoozing almost as soon as I sat down in the train's seat as we pulled away from the station in Leeds.

With a twitch and a snort, I woke up as the train pulled into York's rail station. I felt slightly refreshed, and delighted to finally be at our intended destination.

In York, we meandered from the rail station towards city centre, with our suitcases bumping along the cobbled pavement in the dark, through city centre, up and down some streets outside the city walls, meeting up with non-passable flooded areas, which led to some backtracking of our steps. We considered a couple places to inquire at for lodging, but decided to pass on the ones that we first saw, as the rental rates were a little steep, or the lodgings looked a little too much like a motel.

44 Queen Anne's Road held our attention, though. The building was a friendly looking Tudor, with windows all throughout the front, and a sign which read: "Vacancy." This looked interesting, and we found that at the off-season rate of twenty pounds per person per night for a cozy, en-suite establishment, this place, called St. Raphael Guest House, was just what we had hoped to find.

St. Raphael's has eight letting rooms, and is self-described as "A small family-run guest house, with a homely atmosphere, only five minutes walk from the city centre." One of the proprietors, Janet, had met our ringing of the house's doorbell, and she had shown us a room that was available.

Janet has a hurried manner about her, business-like, but accommodating. She gave us our key to the room and a key to the outside door, she said that she was about to go out for the evening with her husband, Steve, and we might have to wiggle the key to the outside door a little to get back in, but the key will work. We tested the key and found it to work just fine. If we need anything, she mentioned, they'd be back late, but would help us out as they could.

We unpacked, settled in a bit, and noticed that St. Raphael's seemed to be vacant except for the two of us as we headed out the door, tested the lock, and walked back into city centre. It was nice to be back on familiar ground again, in a town that I recognized, and more so for Bill.

Bill has made many trips to England over the past half dozen years, and each trip to England requires a stay in York, as he has a business associate in this city. On my one previous trip to England with Bill, we had stayed in York for a few days and I found it to be a wonderful place. There are walls circling the city, some parts of the walls date back to Roman times, almost two thousand years ago, when this city was called *Eboracum*. The name, York, derives from the days of the Vikings, when the community was named Jorvik. That old Viking scoundrel, Ivan the Boneless, captured the city on the first day of November, 866. I don't mention Ivan for any real reason aside from the fact that he has a moniker that is worth referring to. York has a population of around 100,000 people; it's small enough to get comfortable in rather quickly, yet large enough to get lost in (rather quickly, also, if a person isn't careful; the maze of streets can be confounding at times).

We were both eager to unpack, and to get out into city centre for a bit, and also to unwind from our rail travel by doing a short pub crawl.

We stopped into a pub, The Roman Baths, where I had a pint of the best hand- poured-cask-conditioned-ale I've tasted since May of 1998 on my previous visit to York: a John Smith's Extra Smooth Bitter. It was good enough to have a second pint. Not far away is the Last Drop Inn, where they offer Centurion Ghost Ale, Yorkshire Terrier, and

Hoegaarden (I should have tried a Hoegaarden, just for the name). A poster was up, advertising a guitar/string bass duo, *The String Dazzlers* for Monday night entertainment.

Nearing nine o'clock, we went to The Northern Wall – this pub featured the same stomping disco music and videos on the large screen television as on my last visit to York, but we had a couple half pints of Guinness, anyway, then set out to find the Red Lion. The Red Lion is an old, old pub. Centuries old. Low, low ceilings, and a busy place. It's easy to imagine the chortling masses as they partook of some ales by the fireplace all those years ago. Both feeling somewhat full of ale, though, we limited ourselves to a half-pint of John Smith's apiece, but enjoyed the Red Lion's atmosphere very much.

We then headed back towards Bootham to sample what the Flaming Hot Takeaway had to offer. I ordered sweet & sour Chicken Dhansak for £3.80. The two of us were the larger part of the customers frequenting this takeaway at the time we were there; still we had a considerable wait until our food was ready. We brought our food back to the B&B, scarfed our meals down (they were excellent, with a good amount of spices), and I was reminded in the wee hours why I try to avoid spicy, heavy meals late in the evening.

CHAPTER EIGHT

The Medieval City of York

The Chicken Dhansak had gurgled around enthusiastically inside of me Saturday night and into early Sunday morning. My time awake in the middle of the night left me feeling a little groggy in the morning; I was happy to have woken up a little later than usual, but not too late to relish the prospect of a hearty breakfast.

I looked at our room as I got ready for the day. Even with suitcases and articles of clothing scattered about, the room was more than agreeable. The walls sported light colored wallpaper with a diamond design, the furniture was of good quality, and the storage spaces had ample room for our belongings. The carpeting was of a pleasing design, and the coverings on the beds were plentiful, though just a little bit on the frilly side. The bathroom was clean and tidy, with a plentiful supply of soap and shampoo. We even had a ceramic dog companion between our beds, a Corgi, I believe. I almost hated to part ways with our room that Sunday morning, but I was ready for a full English breakfast, and

Bill and I were to find the breakfast room as delightful as anything we had encountered here previously.

There were pictures of horses everywhere, and more ceramic dogs. We placed ourselves at a table closest to the front windows, and next to a small-scale ceramic Springer Spaniel obeying his command to *stay* on a window's ledge.

The tables were decorated in white linen, the matching plates, cups, and bowls were obviously not purchased at a bargain discount house, houseplants were stationed around the room, and there was a cereal bar with a selection of four starters that could make one scratch his neck in wonderment. I know I did when I set eyes on it.

The scent of the room was one of a fantastic breakfast in the works. This was going to be good.

I decided on orange juice with crispy rice cereal to push my appetite into moving along in the right direction, even more than it was. Janet, the proprietor of the B&B, followed this up with sausages, an egg, toast, and three mushroom tops. Bacon and a tomato were available, also, but I declined the offer for this extra nourishment. This was the finest breakfast yet on this trip. Although I had become accustomed to a larger portion of mushrooms, I was more than satisfied, eupeptic, and ready to take on the day.

Before setting foot in England, I was thinking that I'd like to head up to Thirsk for a day, and possibly even overnight. Thirsk was the home to one of my heroes, Alf Wight. Mr. Wight, or James Herriot, as he is better known, wrote a series of tomes about his experiences as a Yorkshire veterinarian in his *All Creatures Great and Small* collection of books. He had a way of telling a tale that was unsurpassed, and brought an enormous amount of local flavor to his stories of tending to ailing animals in and around the town that he named Darrowby in his books. Darrowby is actually a combination of Yorkshire towns and had its roots in Thirsk, around twenty miles northwards of York.

Bill was agreeable to visiting Thirsk, also. We had made a short visit there on our previous England visit, and we had each had a glass of ale at the Darrowby Inn and visited the town's tourist information office. At that time, in 1998, there were donations being solicited for the building of a museum to honor their famous vet. We had each donated several pounds, and we were interested to find out how the museum, "The World of James Herriot" had turned out.

After strolling to the York rail station and checking on the Sunday rail service to Thirsk, we found that there were no trains running to Thirsk on Sundays. A bus ride would be an alternate way to travel, but we found that Thirsk was not on any Sunday bus routes, either. Both the trains and the busses rallied off in every direction but the one that we cared to go to. Well, then. We'd just have to think about something else to do to occupy our time on a Sunday, and save Thirsk for Monday.

Walking around York, we had a saunter down the Shambles. The Shambles is a picturesque street, almost like something out of a theme park, but it's all real, and all old. The street is narrow, and the ancient buildings along the street almost reach out to rest against the passersby. At one time, the Shambles was the butchering center of York, and word has it that rivers of blood from the slaughtered animals would course down the street, ankle deep. It's been cleaned up a bit since those days, though.

We came upon and wandered around York's outdoor Newgate Market for a while in the mid-morning. I bought a 50p paperback about regional wildlife in the Peak District and a four-pack of AA batteries, which were attractively priced at £1.00, for my camera; the camera had stopped cooperating with me just before we got to the market. After replacing the camera's batteries, I found that the new batteries were good for exactly one picture. One pound, one picture. *Hmmph.*

Margaret Clitherow used to live around here. Margaret is long gone, though a memorial remains. In the 1500's she had helped to sneak priests into and out of York, and the law took a dim view of this practice. Her punishment, as she had decided to neither enter a plea of "guilty" or "not guilty" to these charges, was to have a tremendous door placed upon her body, with large, heavy stones arranged upon the door until the very life was crushed out of her.

Pressing on, but in a preferable manner, Bill and I went straight on to the Castle Museum, which was to open at 11 AM. We were first in line at the museum, but the slight, gray-haired woman at the ticket booth would hardly look at us. When I asked for a ticket, she said softly, with thin, pursed lips, "Two more minutes." I checked my watch. It was only 10:58.

Bill was standing behind me, and conspired in a low voice, "Tell her, 'Oh, gee whiz, lady, give us a break, let us in a couple minutes early!'" I snickered, and I was shot a glance by this ticket woman who said without words that she had a serious job, and there was to be no tomfoolery while she was on duty. I composed myself, and tried to avoid her stare for what seemed like much longer than two minutes.

Once 11:00 rolled around, we were free to pay our £5.25 and get in to see the sights. York's Castle Museum has recreations of 19th century rooms, a mouthwatering display of England's history of chocolates, along with prison rooms (one with a less than inviting steel bed that prisoners on death row would sleep on), suits of armor, World War II displays, and recreations of Victorian streets and storefronts. Bill and I became separated somewhere in there, in the area of the late 1800's streets and shops.

After a couple hours of wandering around, I looked for Bill one last time, and decided that he must have already left the museum, and we would most likely meet up again later in the day. I wasn't overly concerned, as Bill knows the city well. Besides, I held our sole set of keys to St. Raphael's in my pocket. I went out the museum's doors, and across the street to climb the fifty or so steps to Clifford's Tower, across the street from the museum. Clifford's Tower is the remains of an old castle where York's population of Jews sought refuge before being burned to death in a massacre in 1190.

I ambled around the streets of York for awhile, half-wondering where Bill could have ended up, and I found an Internet café, part of the same chain that we had encountered in Cardiff and I boasted a membership card. I sent an email or two, and checked my local St. Paul, Minnesota on-line newspaper (I found that there was nothing going on back home that couldn't wait until I returned). Now, who was to walk into this Internet café, but Bill! He had tried to backtrack at the museum to find me, but he had no luck at that. We arranged to meet back at the B&B later in the afternoon, and he left to wander the city's streets and the narrow connecting pathways (*snickleways*), and to stop into a baker's shop for a 16p sausage roll.

Finishing up on the computer terminal, I remembered this time to have my customer card validated.

By this time, it was mid-afternoon, and I was famished.

Looking for lunch, I found a red-hued building with a sign reading: "Scott the Pork Butchers," and underneath that, another sign: "York Hams Bacon Lard." On the window was an advertisement for hot sandwiches for £1.95, and further below that was another sign, which boasted the variety of hot sandwiches available.

This looked intriguing. The rain was beginning to humble my spirits, but a hot sandwich would pick me back up again. I stepped into the brightly-lit shop, and ordered a pork, stuffing, and applesauce sandwich along with two small, but generous, 30p apple pies. There was no seating available, so I packed my bagged lunch inside my jacket to keep it out of the elements and stepped back outside.

The weather had turned out to be nasty, windy, and rainy after a sunny start in the morning. Walking though city centre, though Bootham Bar back towards the St. Raphael's, the wind turned my umbrella inside out, and I had to do a bit of juggling in an attempt to keep my head dry and my lunch half warm and not too damp.

Through the rain, I saw a Mexican special advertised in a window at a restaurant on my way back to the B&B. Wondering how late they were open, and thinking this might possibly be a place to eat dinner later on, I poked my head into the establishment and queried a waiter.

"How late are you open?"

"Excuse me?"

"What time do you close?"

"Oh…Half ten."

"What?" I cocked my ear.

"Half ten."

"Ok. Thanks."

10:30 PM is closing time, I decided, after mulling his response around in the space of a few blocks of dank walking towards the bed and breakfast.

I thought that I'd find Bill back at St. Raphael's by the time I got there, but he hadn't arrived yet, so I dried myself off as best as I could, sat on my bed, ate my pork sandwich and tried to take a short mid-afternoon nap. Thoughts of a dog kept creeping into and swirling around in my mind, though. While in city centre, I saw a wet, bedraggled dog with hunched shoulders and head hung low. This black and white Border Collie surely was a prized companion from the way he stood at his master's side while braving the elements. I wished that I had taken a picture, as the dog looked remarkably like my Border Collie mix at home, Sadie, who was having her own vacation with her two animal housemates out in a countryside kennel back in Minnesota. I needed to get out again. I scribbled a short note explaining my intended whereabouts to Bill, and I was out the door again to see what mischief I could land myself in.

The rain had let up, and I made my way past St. Mary's Tower, and back towards Bootham Bar to take the stone steps up to the medieval walls. This area, in days long ago, was where the ancient Forest of Galtres and its wolves extended to nearly the city walls.

York's walls nearly encircle the city centre, and have been standing for centuries. Some old fusspots, in the early part of the 19th century, thought that the walls should be taken down, as the walls were anti-quated, and they were becoming too expensive to keep maintained. Portions of the walls were destroyed, including four gates, before the York Footpath Committee was formed, who stepped in to argue the cause for leaving the walls up. There were hindrances to keeping the walls. It was said that the walls had no particular historical interest about them, and, as the walls didn't allow for circulation of air within the city, they promoted ill health to the residents of York.

I thought a little stroll on these walls to look at the city (and to gulp down some breezy air) would be a nice diversion, but I was a little unsure when they would lock the walls up, as there was a sign saying the walls were secured at dusk. I kept my walk short, as it was nearing sun-down; I was uneasy about the possibility of being immured on a possibly inclement November night. I went back down Bootham Bar's stone steps to get back to street level and to take a short walk to the Minster.

Bootham Bar is one of several gateways that lead a person into the city of York. It is on the north end of the city, and closest to the bed and breakfast that we stayed at. South of the city is Micklegate Bar, and off to the eastern sides of city centre are Monk Bar and Walmgate Bar. In olden times these stone arches, with their keepers, would bar a person from straying into or out of the city. Today, one of the bars, Monk, still has a working portcullis; it was Micklegate, the monarch's entrance, which was one of the main display point of traitor's severed heads for all to see, as a warning to be good lest your head be lopped off, stuck up on a stick, and the parasites would infest your noggin for years to come.

It's nice to think about those fine old times. The Minster was there for all that. It's been there for a lot of years. The first Minster was built in the 600's. The cathedral that is on the site today was built between the years 1220 and 1472. Imagine that. It took over two hundred and fifty years to build a church. And yet, as Bill has reminded me, it was still completed some twenty years before Columbus set foot in America. Those were some dedicated construction workers that gave their time and energy to get this building ship-shape. There are outstanding stained glass windows, fine carvings, magnificent tombs, and a sense of awe as a one enters into the church. The echoes of my footsteps in my cheap walking shoes took on an almost spiritual tone as I clopped my way towards the nave, and I heard a priest's voice rising through the building and reverberating about the surroundings.

I was hoping to tour the Minster, however, there was a Sunday service going on at that time, so the majority of the cathedral was blocked off to tourists. There are folding chairs that the churchgoers can sit upon, and the seating was far from full. I thought it would be less imposing to sit on one of the stone benches off towards a wall, along with the other tourists, and enjoy the choir's hymns, which had just begun.

I sat there for awhile, until the service ended. The parishioners began to file out, and I headed towards the gift shop to see what good stuff I could find to take home. I browsed around through the pens, pencils, plastic doo-dads, and so on, all emblazoned with a souvenir etching of the Minster on each piece. The church choir was walking out at this time, and the boys were having a grand time after their uplifting performance. Cackles of laughter, shouting, and overall pre-adolescent mayhem were the rule as the youngsters made their way past the gift shop; an older adult voice kept hushing, "Boys! *Shh! Shhhhhhh!!!*" Now what were these rapscallions thinking, having a good-hearted laugh inside a church? Don't they know about how solemn they're supposed to act in the presence of all this magnificence? I'd suppose the choir has been filing out for centuries, under the same circumstances. My best guess is that they were talking about Grape Lane, only a couple streets down from the Minster. Grape Lane has had its name changed over the years. This short, narrow, street was known at one time as Grapcunt Lane, *grap* being an old-time way of way of spelling *grope*; around the time of the 1300's this was the place in town to skirt a puddle or two and meet a lady of the evening.

As the ruckus died off, I decided to buy a small, glass picture of a Border Collie, handmade; I paid, and went out the Minster's front way (a heavy wooden door, where a person should duck so as to not knock his head on the framing above).

I turned left, and went up a street called Deangate, and then to St. William's College, built in the mid-1400's. After giving the building a thorough looking over, I poked my head into a few neighborhood stores, and then went back to the B&B where I met up with Bill to discuss the evening's plans.

We looked through York's listing of what's on, thinking about the possibility of taking in a movie this evening or perhaps being spirited away on one of York's ghost walk tours. Either event sounded pleasant, but we looked further into the evening's entertainment options, and decided to set our sites toward Cumberland Street, and the York Grand Opera House. There was a one-night only performance of Abba Gold – a tribute band to our pals, Abba, who had provided the musical inspiration for the play we had seen in London. Those Abba tunes are catchy, and we couldn't get enough of them.

It was £12.50 for dress circle seats (one balcony lower than the top balcony), and the girl at the ticket office was a little surprised when I asked if there were still tickets available for the show a half-hour before show time. We bought our tickets, headed out the door, turned to the left, and then turned to the right, and walked back into the ticket booth to ask where the door to the Opera House is located. Of course, it was the opposite way that we thought it might be. We found the Opera House entrance, realized we had time for a half pint, and found a pub, O'Neill's, to wait it out until the show began.

O'Neill's is a well-lit pub, with painted walls and a wooden floor. I tried the Caffrey's, and Bill had a Guinness.

Abba Gold ("As Swedish as Volvo") was a fine diversion for the evening. It wasn't the finest concert I've ever been to (some of the music seemed to be pre-recorded), but the ladies who sang had good voices, the guitar player passed well enough for the real Abba's guitarist, and the keyboard player had taken the time to cut up what looked to be duct tape, and place it neatly on the side of his piano, to form the name "ABBA" in large, bold silver letters. Their Swedish accents took on a little bit of English intonations at times, but the row of girls in front of us had a great time. I guess I did, too, but not nearly as great a time as these young girls did.

This group of eight to twelve year olds sang and danced along to their favorites: "Dancing Queen," "S.O.S.," "Voulez-Vouz," and all the other hits. A mid-30's blonde mom-chaperone was having almost as good a time. At the interval, there was ice cream to be purchased. As Bill had bought the round of ice cream at the theater in London, I bought it here in York. The young man with the tray of ice cream was most apologetic when he gave me my change. The smallest note I had to pay him with was a tenner, and he had change in mostly 50p coins. "Sorry," he said, several times over.

We enjoyed the rest of the show, and then walked back towards St. Raphael's B&B, stopping into a green grocer for some snacks. I got a 33p carton of milk and some digestives (digestives are a great little snack – round, sweet, fiber-rich cookies) to go with my apple pie that I had saved from earlier in the day. Bill had purchased some snacks, also, but I was feeling a little generous, so I offered my second apple pie to him, although I hogged the milk for myself, which was fine with Bill, as I was drinking straight from the carton.

CHAPTER NINE

Thirsk

I like to go for a run. At home, I try my best to get out for at least a short run most days of the week, taking my two dogs with me to get in some fresh air and exercise. I had good intentions on this trip to get out for a jog most mornings before breakfast, but so far, those plans had been laid to waste. I hadn't brought my running togs along to let them sit in my suitcase unused and smelling fresh, though. On this Monday morning, I decided that I had better get back in action, so I woke myself early. It was a fine, clear morning. I scrubbed up, changed, stretched, and got myself out the door.

I jogged down Bootham, turned left onto Gillygate, past the street's Georgian buildings, looped around, and then went into city center via Bootham Bar. I saw the reflected sun rise on the Minster as I ran by, from what a plaque says, where the Queen once visited. I ran across the Lendal Bridge, saw the crowds going to work, and spotted the woman who chaperoned the young girls at the previous night's show (at least I thought it was her). I toured the city on my running shoes, and then I was back to St. Raphael's to shower and have a full English breakfast (minus one strip of bacon, which I smuggled into a napkin and stuck in my pocket for later, in case I needed a quick sustenance).

It was Monday already. Most Mondays I might feel a sense of slight dread at having to face another week at work (oh, I like my job, but there are other things that a person could really be doing to occupy the hours between Monday and Friday). This was the last day that our Britrail Weekender passes were valid, and I had plans to go up to Thirsk for part of the day if the rail lines were operating (otherwise, I'd settle for bus travel, if that was available), and Bill still needed to meet with his friend, Jonathan, to discuss business transactions. After our separate plans, we would make an attempt to hook up to get on the same south-bound train to go back to London to honor our previously made reservations at the Georgian House Hotel, back in London.

We paid our bill at St. Raphael's, and inquired if we could leave our suitcases there until later in the afternoon (the proprietor said it was fine to do that), then we made our morning trek down Bootham and past a little black vehicle that we had seen parked along the street several times previously. This runt of a car, called a Smart Car, is eight feet in length from front headlights to back taillights, gets outstanding gas mileage, and looks like it would be a whole lot of fun to drive.

Sadly, though, we weren't inside a Smart Car, we were hoofing it again. And we hoofed it into city centre, where we stopped into Jonathan's place of business, a blue-tinted building just inside the city walls. Saying a quick hello, Bill explained what we were up to: the two of us were going to walk down to the rail station and check on the train schedules to and from Thirsk. Most likely I would be in Thirsk for a few hours, Bill would go back to meet with Jonathan, and I would be back in York later on in the day. Jonathan's reaction to my plans to visit this small Northern Yorkshire town was one of astonishment, as Bill told me later on. Jonathan wondered why one would want to go to Thirsk, even for a few hours. I suppose if one is too close to something good for a number of years, one gets used to it, and hardly even pays attention to it, and may not even give it the nod that it deserves.

At the rail station, it was 10:20 when we found that there was a train for me to Thirsk, which would depart at 10:27 on platform 8; there would be a return train leaving Thirsk for York at 1:40. Bill jotted down the time that I expected to back in York, then I had to get a move on. I hurried up a staircase, and then down a staircase, crossing the tracks, to what I thought was platform 8. I was just about to hurl myself onto the train, when I thought maybe I had better check with someone, lest I wind up not where I expected to be. The conductor was right there, and he assured me I was about to board the correct train. I jumped on the train with barely any time to spare, as the conductor's whistle sounded seconds after I took my seat, and the train chugged out of the station.

This was exciting. I had become accustomed to relying on my older brother's advice and travel knowledge over the past several days, and mostly following in his footsteps as we toured England and Wales. Now I was venturing out to do some exploring on my own, and I was thrilled. Any wrong turns, if I were to make them, would belong to just myself. I had the foresight, though, to take along the phone number to Jonathan's shop, just in case I should need it.

It was a slow, crawling train ride at first. This was one of the first trains to go north out of York after the floods. We'd creep along, build up a little speed, then slow back down again. There were only two other people in this car; I wondered if they thought the same as me—if we might have been getting there a little faster if we had been walking. Once we were over a recently flooded bridge, we picked up speed again, and kept moving along at a good clip, past the green, water-laden pastures of Yorkshire. It was good and warm on the train. The heat was working well; I took off my jacket and rolled up my shirtsleeves.

I was the sole person to get off the train at its first stop, Thirsk. Thirsk has a small train station, a little bigger than a good-sized ice-fishing shack. I had a quick look around at the melancholy surroundings (typical of a November Monday morning, I surmised), and inquired at the ticket window to make sure there was an early afternoon train back to York. The man at the window confirmed that the scheduled service was at 1:40 to York and I was satisfied. I spied a sign pointing me to the heart of town. I took off, walking down Station Road towards The World of James Herriot Museum. Or so I was hoping. It seemed like the likely direction to walk in, and it felt right.

On one side of me was a pasture of sheep and goats; on the other side of the road were industrial looking buildings, a few well-kept houses scattered about, a livestock auction yard, and a Ford car sales lot. This walk was taking a little longer than I had anticipated, and I was growing a little curious if I had read the rail station's directional sign correctly.

As I neared the town's horse racing track, I saw an older woman, carrying shopping bags, and walking towards me a couple football field lengths away. Once I got near enough, I noticed that she was bundled up in a long coat and had a scarf over her hair. I asked her if I was walking the correct way to get to the Herriot Museum.

"Yes."

She paused.

"Yes, yes." That was the end of her reply, as she nodded down the road in the direction I was heading towards and she began to walk, once more, on her way. I thanked her.

Ten minutes later, around a few curves, and past a small cinema, I was in city centre and in the town's market, next to Thirsk's clock tower. I sat on a bench near the clock tower to survey the town for a few minutes. I liked what I saw: small shops, with varying façades, nesting up against one another along a cobbled pavement, the outdoor market was doing brisk business, and the populace looked to be enjoying their Monday morning routines. I flapped my jacket to dispel some sweat, then jumped up to go around the corner to 23 Kirkgate—Skeldale House, and The World of James Herriot.

The building is cheerful, constructed of red bricks, with white painted trim framing the windows and a green sign out front advertising the nature of the enterprise. Healthy green vines crawl up and decorate the walls, while potted flowers in a wooden tub outside the front door encourage one to pause for a moment to take a picture of the setting.

After purchasing my ticket at the tourist information building next door, I approached the vets' former residence with camera still in hand. The door was open, I took a picture, and the resonance surrounding me was a deep, hearty Yorkshire accent.

"Do you want me to close the door so you can get a better picture?"

"No, thanks. That was just what I wanted," I offered.

This helpful gent escorted me into Skeldale House and gave me a brief run though of what to expect at the museum. He also verified my ticket, then sent me off on my way to the surroundings with a resounding, "Take as many pictures as you want!" I half expected him to give me a good-natured clap on the shoulder as I left his company.

Two and a half years earlier, I passed through Thirsk with Bill when this museum was in the design stage, and the tourist information centre was across the street in a ramshackle room, with a plea for donations to help build the museum. Both Bill and I donated some pounds to the cause, and the donations they received from all their supporters have been well used.

As I took in the *All Creatures Great and Small* setting, the one-time home of James, Siegfried, and Tristan, I realized that it all seemed much smaller than I had expected. The front door led me directly into a hallway, with the living room, which doubled as a bill-paying room for the Yorkshire farmers once a month, just to the right. The telephone that James Herriot would rush down the stairs to answer in the middle of the night was only a few feet from the living room. The small dispensary was to the left, and the kitchen, with its scullery, was steps ahead, down the narrow hall.

The furnishings were restorations of 1940's–50's style rooms, and close to how they would have looked when the house was occupied by Yorkshire's famous vet. The radios were tuned to Bing Crosby and to war news. Walking out through the back door, I delighted in the wisteria that climbs up the building, but focused on the 1937 Austin Seven car parked by the garden, with the license plate number AJO 71. This was the exact same vehicle used in episodes of the *All Creatures Great and Small* television series. A sign and an open driver's side door invited visitors to sit in the old car, and I wasn't about to let an opportunity like this slip by me. I took my place in the driver's seat, regretted that the keys had been removed, but imagined myself backing the Austin Seven out of the driveway, being careful not to hit anything that I'd have to pay for. It was fun. I got out, tossed a few loose coins in the fountain near the car, and headed into the tack house to look at some old horse equipment.

The tack house was worth a quick look for me. A horse enthusiast could most likely spend extra time in there, looking at all the old paraphernalia. I headed to the next section of this self-guided tour: a recreation of a farmer's foldyard, outfitted similar to how a vet would have seen it years ago, as he gave help to ailing livestock. Inside the foldyard there was an enjoyable fifteen minute movie about the life of Alf Wight (the vet's actual name) on a large screen television in the foldyard, including a talk show snippet that featured the vet himself, speaking in his—not Yorkshire accent—but Glaswegian manner of speaking (Alf Wight spent his formative years in Glasgow, Scotland).

I was glad I still had my morning bacon in my pocket; I was ready for a snack. I pulled a surplus of necessities out of my pockets, items that I had stashed away for the day, before I recognized the greasy napkin where my snack waited for me. There was a couple in their mid 60's in the foldyard who were also watching the movie. They gave me glances out of the corners of their eyes and cleared their throats while I rustled around, pulling items out of my pockets and stuffing them away again. As I started munching on my slice of bacon, I heard a throat clearing again and then a sigh. They must have been downhearted because they didn't think to bring along a snack like I did.

At the movie's end, I hurried out the foldyard door, giving a quick smile to the couple with whom I had shared the movie. I hoped that my flashing of teeth would send a message saying that I was sorry I hadn't brought enough bacon for everybody. I was beginning to feel a little pressed for time, and I wanted to have a look through the museum's other exhibits, visit its gift shop, as well as walk around town afterwards, if there was still time before my train was scheduled to depart.

The BBC set of the television series is recreated at the museum, and merits a visit. Cameras, lights, and monitors are on display, along with actual sets of the sitting room and dispensary. These scenes looked a little more familiar to me than the actual house. I could see the similarities, though. A phone rang incessantly while I was in this exhibit, and I was about to pick up its receiver to make the room a little quieter, but I decided to move on instead. I found out later that if I had picked up the phone there was a good chance that the voice of a distressed Yorkshire farmer would have been on the other end of the line, asking to have a vet come look at some unwell livestock.

Upstairs is a *visible animal* exhibit where a person can have a look inside various model animals; there is also a display of old veterinary weapons, ahhh…I mean instruments, and a loo. On the way out, I picked up a couple of souvenirs downstairs at the gift shop. The cashier at the shop asked what I thought of the museum. "It was wonderful, I could have stayed here twice as long," I replied. And I meant it. Of course I would have needed extra bacon in my pockets for a visit any longer than it was

The slight drawback was that I was hoping to see the entire house made into a recreation of the residence, not just the ground floor, but I was more than satisfied.

Making the short walk to city centre, I stopped off at a bank's cash point. I was curious to find out if my debit card would work in England.

I assumed that it would, but I hadn't yet had to use the card; I would prefer finding out that it doesn't work before I need to use it, rather than when I'm down to my last one pound coin. As the machine was processing my £20.00 transaction, there was a polite notice that flashed up on the screen: "Please wait while we are dealing with your request."

It didn't take long at all to deal with my request. This amazed me. Here I was, in a small Yorkshire town, and this machine's computer had to talk to the computer that keeps tabs on my credit union deposits and withdrawals way over in the United States.

I had the equivalent of twenty pound's worth of money go whirring out of my account in the Midwest just several seconds later, then ending up in my hands as a twenty-pound note.

It's truly amazing, especially when I think that my card seems to not work half the time when I'm simply trying to pick up a six-pack of beer on the way home from work in the evening.

I walked through the outdoor market, and stopped into James Herriot's *Drovers Arms*, the pub that is mentioned throughout his books. The Drovers Arms is actually a hotel by the name of The Golden Fleece with a pub inside. I thought that it might be fun to pick up a souvenir matchbox with "The Golden Fleece" printed on it. I walked into the hotel, turned left to get to the dark, wood-laden bar, and asked the bartender for matches. I received a box of matches with the "Best Western" logo on it. Ah well…times change. It was a nice pub, though. I would have liked to have stayed to relish a mid-day ale if I had given myself ten minutes less at the museum.

As it was, a visit to the grocery store, a few doors down from the Golden Fleece would be not as enjoyable as having an ale, but more practical for the afternoon. I was going to have to take my walk back to the rail station soon, and I thought a bottled soft drink would hit the spot very well.

Along with a Dr. Pepper, I picked up the local newspaper, the *Darlington & Stockton Times*. The cash register attendant was more than a little surprised at how much stuff I had to dig out of my pockets to come up with less than a pound in change to pay for my purchase. So was I. It's amazing how much can be accumulated in less than a day. With each handful of doodads that I dug out, the cashier's eyebrows would rise up one notch higher than the previous time. Another customer, who seemed to be a long-time acquaintance of the cashier, stood behind me, waiting his turn, and exchanging perplexed half-grins with the clerk. I was happy that the bacon was long gone.

Thirsk is an agreeable town. The people are friendly, they say hello to each other on the street, and they don't mind giving a person a hard time if it takes too long to drag a few coins out of his pocket. I was back up the road, though, swigging my bottled beverage, walking past the Ritz Theater and towards the sheep and goats who got a neighborly nod and goodbye from me as I passed them on my way to the rail station.

I checked with the rail attendant once I got back to the station to make sure I was on time for the train back to York.

"I told you the train was leaving for York at 1:40 because it's actually a 1 PM train, but it's running late. I figured you'd get either the 1 PM train or be early for the 2 PM train." He was right. The 1 PM train was late, but ironically on time as well.

At 1:38 the keeper of the rail station locked up his building, waited on the north side of the platform from me, and the train arrived right on its belated schedule, two minutes later. The attendant hopped onto the same train to York that I was setting foot on. It was another small batch of train travelers. The station attendant was on the car in back of me, and there was one other person in my car. I took off my jacket to air out from the cool dampness of northern Yorkshire, and we slowed down to less than a crawl to head over the bridge back to York.

CHAPTER TEN

Train to London

Back in York, I had a swift walk over the Lendal Bridge, huffing and puffing through the city's maze of streets, as I tried to make time in order to get back to Bill's friend's shop. The time was going to be tight; earlier in the day, we had discussed catching the next train to London once I was back in town, and the time was growing near to that train's departure. I wiped the sweat from my brow as I knocked on Jonathan's door. There would be only enough time to say a quick greeting, gather Bill, walk speedily up Bootham towards St. Raphael's, where our suitcases were stowed, then make haste back to the train station. The schedule was going to be strained, but we could make it if we hurried. I waited only seconds until one of the shopkeepers answered my knock.

We exchanged hellos, and she directed me towards the room where Bill and Jonathan were. I had half-expected Bill to have his jacket on, pacing the floor in an agitated way, waiting for me.

That was not the case, though. The two of them were leisurely discussing what had happened in their lives since their last meeting, and it took a moment until they realized I was in the room with them. Jonathan, in his relaxed manner, offered me a chair, and inquired how my day was. The discussion led to this and that, and before too long, Bill suggested that we would probably not have enough time to catch the next train to London, "Maybe we should just wait and take the train that will be leaving York later in the day."

I had grown a little perplexed as to why I had hurried as much as I had. York is a fine little city, I was in pleasant company, and I wouldn't mind spending an extra hour or so here before moving on to London. With the swift two-hour train ride from York to London, we'd still be back in London by six PM.

Jonathan inquired about my tastes in beer, and how I was enjoying the local brews. I am of the opinion that an English hand poured cask conditioned ale is one of the finest beverages around, and I told of the beer selection that I had sampled in the finest terms, and lamenting that I had yet to discover anything comparable back home in Minnesota.

"Before flying out of Minnesota," I mentioned, "I picked up an eight-pack of tins of Guinness to have something sort of close to a hand poured cask conditioned ale once I got home."

"Eight?" Jonathan questioned.

"Well, you can never have enough good beer in the refrigerator."

The conversion lulled as Jonathan took this information in. I felt my mind growing blank at how to follow this up, as all remained silent for an insufferable amount of time.

My attention turned as Jonathan looked straight at Bill and asked, "How is your wife? Is she *all right*?"

I had an unanticipated inner turmoil. Bill had made daily phone calls back home to talk to his wife. I had thought that Bill was just checking in. Maybe something was wrong that he wasn't letting on about. I glanced apprehensively between the two of them. Bill hesitated, then rolled his eyes, grinned, and said that his wife was never better, and talked glowingly for some time about her.

I rested my chin on my hand, and pursed my lips as I remembered that when a person from this part of the world asks if someone is all right, this sounds ominous, but it is what we in the Midwest would phrase as something like, "How's the wife?" A simple inquiry.

After more unhurried discussion, which led more and more towards Bill and Jonathan's common interests, I was growing antsy. After what seemed like quite a while (which it might have been, but it was probably less than a quarter of an hour), Bill looked at the watch on his wrist, and said that maybe we had better move on to pick up our suitcases at St. Raphael's.

I was fine with that. I don't know Jonathan well, but I think he's a fine sort of person. I didn't want to give the impression that I was trying to get away from his company, but I was looking forward to heading back to the B&B in London, settling in again, and having a couple of the beers we had talked of earlier, as well as relishing a hearty dinner.

We tinkered with the idea of having one last beer in York for an afternoon's send-off, but the general thought was that it might be a better use of our time to go back to pick up our belongings and head to the train station to make sure that we did, indeed, catch the next train bound for London. Our suitcases were inside the breakfast room at St. Raphael's, we grabbed them, said a quick hello and goodbye to the owner, Janet, thanking her for stowing our belongings safely away, and we bumped our suitcases along the cobbled way back to the rail station to see how the afternoon's transportation to London was progressing.

After speaking to the agent at the station's information window, we learned that trains south from York to London were still not available, due to the flooding and landslips. We could take a bus, though, from York's rail station to Doncaster. Doncaster is a half-hour closer to London than we were, then we'd transfer to a train at the Doncaster station, which would bring us into London.

We grasped at this opportunity to get back to our intended destination, and asked to be pointed to where the bus would pick us up. We received a halfhearted pointing from the agent, but we got an idea of the general direction in which to walk.

There was still a good twenty minutes until the bus would leave, and neither one of us had eaten lunch yet. There was time to stop into a fast food joint, grab some nourishment, and eat the meal on the bus. Bill ordered a Cajun chicken sandwich, and I decided on a veggie burger with all the trimmings.

The pretty, clean scrubbed teenaged girl that took Bill's order had to ask a couple times what it was that Bill was attempting to order, as she took in his American accent, but she soon got the drift, yelled back to the kitchen what was needed, took his money, and gave him his food.

I waited for a minute or two until the next order taker was available. An insecure lad with dark, greasy hair and a face full of pimples greeted me and gazed slightly beyond my left shoulder. He asked me time and time again what it was that I was ordering, stumbling at his interpretation of what I wanted, as I spoke slower and more deliberately on each attempt to get my veggie burger. Building up the fortitude to look me sort of below the chin, he finally repeated my order back to me, and I had to make only a slight correction. The boy asked the order taker who had served Bill for some advice on what to do next. She rolled her eyes, yelled my order back to the kitchen, and told the lad to collect my money. Bill waited patiently for me, with his fast food bag in hand. I finally got my meal, with a "sorry," and Bill and I headed into the asphalt-covered area of the station, where we found a sign locating the area where the bus would pick up southbound passengers.

All was strangely quiet there.

Having a second, harder, look at the sign that was posted, this sign did, indeed, say that a bus would pick up rail passengers at this exact point, and leave in five minutes from the present time. There was no bus, and there were only a few other people milling around, and they didn't seem to be worried about stepping on to a bus anytime soon.

Bill said that an English custom is to put notices up, but change the plans, and not give redirection to the correct area. That seemed to be what was happening here. We walked towards the front of the train station, where several busses were idling. Asking a driver which bus was taking rail passengers to Doncaster, we found that we had happened upon the correct coach; the driver stowed our suitcases in the baggage compartment, and we boarded the vehicle.

Stepping up into the bus, I noticed that the driver has a good-sized boxy space to himself; a person walks up a slope to get to the seats, where the elevation is fine enough to take in all the sights of the journey.

The bus was not crowded, so Bill and I were able to get a little elbow room as we settled into window seats in separate rows. The both of us rustled around in our paper bags, and drew out our fast food, which had grown cold, but was still good to get into our bellies as a late lunch. I ruminated that fast food help can be the same no matter where a person is, but that if my local chain burger joint back in Minnesota served veggie burgers, especially ones that tasted as good as the one I enjoyed, I might just stop in to eat there more than once a year.

It was dusk as we left York, going out of town past the racecourse and onto the A19. The driver fiddled with the radio dial, which had been tuned to pop music when we boarded the bus. After listening to several radio stations over the next few minutes, at varying volumes, the driver decided that pop music would suit us all for the best as we advanced down the road. He turned the volume down to just loud enough to listen to if a person wanted to do that, and quiet enough to not pay too much attention to the top pop hits if one cared to make an attempt to ignore the incessant beat.

The time passed quickly, or possibly I drifted off into a light slumber after my meal. I looked out the window to see the bright lights of what could only be Doncaster. I had heard that Doncaster was less than a sparkling city, but, as night fell, it looked all right to me.

The bus pulled into the train station, where we were met by a conductor with a look of pained anguish on his face as he flailed his arms
this way and that way, yelling, "Train to London! Train to London!" He
settled on a direction to point in, which was somewhere behind his
back, then started his commotion again, "Train to London! Train to
London!" still flapping his arms like a madman, and giving the occa-
sional chirp on his whistle.

We got the sense that this might be urgent, and maybe we had better
hurry along our way lest we miss our transfer. Everyone that we saw
around us was walking at breakneck intensity, and we were just about to
do the same.

We thought that we'd check on the situation, though.

"Excuse me," Bill asked the conductor, 'Which way is the train to
London?"

"Train to London?" the conductor replied. "That way!" he exclaimed,
waving his right arm towards where passengers were boarding a train a
hundred yards away from us. "You'll have to hurry, though, it's just
about to leave!"

"Which are the first class cars?"

"First class? To the rear of the train, but you won't have time to make
it the first class cars. Get on the first car you see, then walk through the
train to first class!" He bugged his eyes out, puffed his cheeks, blew his
whistle, spun around, and commenced with his clamoring, "Train to
London! Train to London!"

It did seem that this section of our journey was taking on a bit of
uncalled for urgency, but we were happy to oblige and trotted off
towards the train, jumping on with a good twenty seconds to spare
before the train chugged away.

Inside the train car, we surveyed the situation. Every seat was taken,
and nearly every set of eyes in every body in every seat looked up at the
two of us as we contemplated our next move. The only possible thing to
do was to take a deep breath, march briskly towards the rear of the car,

and into the next section, and repeat the process several times until we had reached a first class car.

Never had I heard myself mutter "sorry" so many times. Every body in the aisle seats had at least one knee sticking out into the gangway, and my suitcase seemed to have had contact with the majority of those knees along its route. Occasionally, as the train bumped along, I would try to steady myself against a seat back, but I would typically miss my mark, and lean on a fellow passenger's shoulder or head. This usually led to brief eye contact, and a faint smile would emit from me as I attempted to reassure my fellow passengers that I was a bit on the unsteady side. To further illustrate my point, I would move on, giving anyone nearby a solid thwack on the kneecap with my belongings.

At long last, we made it to a first class car. I nearly expected a swelling orchestral symphony to greet us as the door glided open. A few eyes looked up at us two latecomers, but the only sounds were scattered conversations, the clanking of tableware, and the timbre of the train rolling along the tracks.

CHAPTER ELEVEN

Cell Phones and Vulgar Trolls

This first class rail car from Doncaster to London was packed with passengers, but not quite so bad as what we had encountered in the standard class cars. The going was much easier through these wider aisles as we walked our suitcases to the rear of the car, stowed the bags away, and settled into comfortable seats. Bill sat several rows ahead of me.

My seat was across the aisle from a young quiet well-dressed family clearly on vacation; Dad, Mom, and two grammar school aged youths, a boy and a girl. At their table, the children read while the parents conversed quietly and thoughtfully. What a nice family, I thought. Just ahead of me, and with surprisingly fortunate luck on my part, was a busty brunette wearing a tight low cut sweater. Her seat was across the gangway from my seat, and facing me. I had a good feeling about this leg of the journey, and I could only hope that she dropped things frequently and had to lean over to pick stuff up. We were a quarter of the way nearer to London, which meant that in only an hour and a half we would be at King's Cross Station, and that would mean we would be

80

only a tube ride away from Victoria Station, nearer to our bed and breakfast, and the opportunity to recuperate from this busy day.

An attendant arrived, asking me if I'd like a beverage. A cup of tea would be just the thing I needed to help me drift off into a relaxed state while I waited out the next ninety minutes of travel. I ordered my tea, and in an attempt to amuse myself, I tried looking out the windows, but all was dark, and no scenery was to be found aside from a casual light or two every now and then. Looking to my left, I noticed that the two children were done reading, and they had begun to draw pictures. The dad made a call on his cell phone while the mom admired her brood's artwork. The well-endowed woman ahead of me was reading, and a slightly older, and less chesty woman joined this section of the train, withdrawing a cell phone from her purse as she sat.

There was nothing much going on here; this seemed to be a likely time to move my seat down into a reclined position and get some shut-eye. The seat seemed to go back all right, but a little too far. Getting it to go forward was another task. *Uhh-HEM!* I would hear time and time again as I attempted to get my seat to just the right position for repose. It seemed I was disturbing a gent behind me each time I made the seat lower and the seat clunked into a not quite right position. To get the seat to raise forward again I needed to pull the release lever up AND lift my weight off the seat, which I wasn't getting the hang of any too well. After a few unsuccessful tries and bumping around while hearing *Uhh-HEM!* all the while, I figured out the proper coordination to lift my butt off the seat while at the same time raising the lever. Mechanical items and myself really don't get along some days.

I began to drift off to sleep. From somewhere, off in the distance it seemed, I heard *beep beep boop bap beep.* A cell phone was being dialed. An electronic ring made its way into my ears from a nearby seat. More dialing, more ringing of cell phones. Suddenly half the people in this car were having one-sided conversations: "The train's moving really slowly." "I'm bored." "What's for dinner?" "We must be in the country, I can hardly hear you." "I think I'm going to be late." And on it went. The once-pleasant urchins across from me had transmogrified into screeching, crying vulgar trolls. The family, I had gathered from their conversations (not that I was eavesdropping, I just happened to be within listening range with nothing else to do), had been vacationing in France, Scotland, and England for three weeks and they were about to spend one last night in London before flying home to the U.S. in the morning. Morning was not soon enough for the little girl, as she began demanding, "I want to go home. I want to go home NOW!" Her brother chimed in with his own brand of wailing as the two competed in a volume contest.

I moved my seat up from its reclined position. I was done relaxing for a little while, it seemed. The car that I was in was non-smoking, but I had heard announcements that there was a car behind our car where smoking was encouraged. *Car M*, I believe it was named, and I hoped that it was full of quiet adults. I checked my pocket for cigarettes, finding one or two in there, and made a stop in the toilet before going into Car M. There seemed to be a slight problem with the lock on the toilet, but I figured that as long as the door was shut I should have privacy for a half a minute. The door opened abruptly as I was shaking the last bit of tea out of my system and I was about to zip up. This unanticipated visitor's jaw dropped down, and I suppose mine did, also. The woman offered a quick "sorry" as she snapped the door closed. I fiddled with the lock for a little bit, for future reference; I found that it was, indeed, stuck in the "unlock" position, but after some jiggling around, I got it to work.

In Car M, I talked to a gent a few years older than myself, someone who looked like a businessman of some sort, on his way home after a long day of meetings. He told me that this was the worst possible time to be a tourist on a train in England. The railway organizations were doing track maintenance because of a recent derailment, which had put several people into early graves, and the recent rainstorms and flooding had also made the trains run slowly. Normally, the speed of this train is greater than one hundred miles per hour. He made a guess that tonight's speed was more in the range of forty to fifty miles per hour. We were not likely, he surmised, to get into King's Cross Station until half past eight. This typically less than two-hour train ride will have taken over four hours. That would have normally been enough time to travel from Edinburgh to London rather than half the distance.

This train ride really was dragging out.

Going back to my seat, I caught sight of the woman who had walked in on me in the toilet. We exchanged smiles and hellos, then parted ways.

I had stopped into the baggage section of the car, where I opened my suitcase to reach in and grab the *Darlington & Stockton Times*, which I had picked up in Thirsk. There was some good reading in this newspaper, which kept my attention for quite some time: the Richmond Postmaster at Queen's Road, along with his wife, were handcuffed and robbed, and police would not release the names of the victims. (I have to wonder how many postmasters in Richmond are there on Queen Anne's Road, anyway?) Tesco was told to rethink its plans for a Northallerton store. Mopping up has begun after a week of flood misery. There was discord at the Marsk-In-Swaledale Women's Institute because of the cost of guest speakers and the disallowance of picnic lunches at their meetings. I looked through the classified ads more than once. The housing seemed fairly expensive, but there were one or two small dwellings listed at a moderate price.

The noise level of the car had diminished dramatically as I read. Several people seemed to be dozing, the mobile phone use was not as frequent, and the children to my left were whining a lot more quietly and with less frequency.

I got out of my seat to pass the newspaper onto Bill. I found him with a vacant look in his eyes as he stared into the darkness outside his window. He was ready for a little distraction.

I went back to my seat, expertly lowered the seat back to a slightly reclined position. This elicited only a slight clearing of the throat from the man who was seated behind me. I wasn't really feeling the need for a nap any more, but by reclining my seat back I knew from previous experience that I'd obtain a pleasing vantage point of the ample cleavage not far in front of me.

The lights of suburban London finally began to peek out, and we arrived at the King's Cross Station. All of us who disembarked the train couldn't collect our belongings and step off the train fast enough.

Toting our bags once again, we took the Tube to Victoria Station and from there walked back to the Georgian House Hotel. We had made a reservation for a room here at the time we checked out of the Georgian House several days earlier. We were hoping that, as we were arriving at the B&B much later than we anticipated, a room would still be available. It was well past nine o'clock when we buzzed the doorbell to be let into the lobby. As promised, a room was still reserved for us.

The room was just outside the reception area on the ground floor. Handy, we found, but just a thin wall away from a group of jubilant Italian girls on holiday. We unpacked quickly, but noticed that our ensuite lodging was lacking in one amenity: toilet paper. There was one small roll with only a few sheets left on it. I volunteered to ask at the front desk for a full roll of toilet paper, and I'm afraid I embarrassed the receptionist with my request. Not only was she red-faced about having to talk about toilet paper with a guest, she wasn't at all sure where the supply of delicate articles such as this was kept. She made several inquiries to other employees on the night shift, and each time the phrase "toilet paper" would come to pass her lips, her voice would decrease to a fragile whisper. A few minutes passed until a reserve roll was discovered with the aid of her co-workers. I grabbed the treasure and brought it to the room, threw it in the bathroom, and Bill and I headed out the door for a late dinner.

We went up the street a short distance to the Marquis of Westminster, where we each had a couple pints of John Smith's Best Bitter, and an order of fish and chips with plain peas. There was a jar of Colman's Mustard on the table to liven up the meal.

"Here you are boys!" the gregarious waiter would say as he showed us to our table, gave us our pints, and served us our late dinner. He was thin, middle-aged, and pilgarlic, grinning the friendliest, toothiest smile that anyone could hope for. We were some of the last diners at the restaurant that evening, as they closed at 10PM. The waiter, still smiling, seemed genuinely excited by the fact that we were ready to pay our bill at a few minutes past the hour.

After dinner, we did some shopping at a small Indian green grocer, and headed back to the B&B. I had the bed next to the wall of noisy Italian girls. These girls were enjoying their visit to London and making the most of their waking hours.

CHAPTER TWELVE

A Full Plate

Tuesday dawned, and it would be the last full day in England for Bill and me. The plane would be leaving Wednesday morning, carrying us back home to Minnesota; today would be the day to fit in as much as we could, or cared to, to round out our visit. Bill wanted to visit some antiques markets, and I hoped to see some of the historic places that I had missed on our first round of London touring. The weather forecast was for a bright and clear day, with the high temperature expected to be in the mid-40's Fahrenheit.

Bill had plans for a lazy day of bumming around, seeing if he could find any good prices on old items that he couldn't live without, and taking the day for what it had to offer. Bill has been to London several times, and has seen a good amount of the tourist sights. He's not opposed to visiting attractions again, as there's always something new and interesting to explore, even if it's on a repeat visit. But it's good to get out on one's own (especially after one's had to put up with my snoring in the middle of the night). I don't mind having my own rota, either.

I had brought a yellow highlighting pen along with me, and had spent time the previous evening noting places in my London guidebook that I still wanted to see. The catalog I made for myself was larger than I could manage without trimming away some of the fat, and possibly a little of the meat.

I knew that my first stop would be the Tower of London, and I also had a calling to see the Beatles' exhibit at the British Library. The Cabinet War Rooms were on my to-do list, as was the Imperial War Museum. Old Bailey would be a good mid-day diversion, where I could have a glimpse at some of London's accused criminals having their day on trial. St. Paul's Cathedral, St. Martin-in-the-Fields Church, the National Gallery, and the British Museum all were possibilities for rounding out the day. I had a full plate, and I wasn't sure how much I'd be able or willing to take in, but I'd give it my best shot.

We decided the best thing to do would be to go our separate ways right after breakfast, and meet back at the hotel later in the day.

The first thing I had to do, though, was to weed out a few things in my suitcase. I had noticed the night before that my bag was growing increasingly heavy, and I knew the increased resistance to my tugging at it wasn't solely from my fatigue. I had accumulated a good amount of crap that I really didn't want to bring back home with me, and I hated the thought of acquiring more stuff today, and straining further to lift my suitcase off the ground.

I must have been lugging around one or two fairly good-sized trees inside my suitcase with all the various paper I had stowed away. There were brochures that I thought I needed from places that I didn't visit, and newspapers from London, Cardiff, and York that might be fun to look over once I got home, but the papers would probably just sit in a corner for a year or two until I tossed them into the recycling bin.

After my ten minute blitz of cleaning, I looked at the heap of garbage that I had piled into the room's receptacle, and I was satisfied with a job well done. I had toyed with the idea of discarding the

Darlington-Stockton newspaper that I had picked up in Thirsk, but I decided that that was a treasured possession, and I couldn't bear to part with it. I wanted to keep that paper around to have it on hand to reread once I got hungry for North Riding again after returning home.

The morning's breakfast had the same offerings as our previous breakfasts at the Georgian House Hotel. Why change things up and mess with a winning combination? I imagine the servers must grow weary of serving the same offerings day after day, but I don't think I could get tired of all this good stuff. Bill and I started out with some canned fruit. Peaches and grapefruit were offered again and I scooped up a little of each one. Bill heaped his bowl with grapefruit. He always looks forward to finding canned grapefruit sections at bed and breakfasts in England. He swears that the canned grapefruit in England is much better than the canned grapefruit in the States, and he's disappointed if he doesn't find this favorite of his on the menu.

Cereal was available again, and we each had a bowl of it. Then the main course arrived. My Cumberland sausage was a little overdone, the egg was runny like the other eggs that I had eaten here. (I think the eggs are supposed to be this way, but for the life of me, I can't figure out why, even the white part, though cooked, is runny. I've tried to duplicate these runny eggs at home, for something to do on a weekend morning, but I just can't get the hang of making the recipe.) The toast was perfect, and I ventured to test the orange marmalade on the toast this morning. Orange marmalade has never been on my list of favorite things to eat, but I thought that I'd try the brand that was available, and it was passable. I made the decision to opt out of the bacon this morning, and, to balance the scales, I received a more than ample portion of mushrooms.

We were both stuffed, and we each set off for our own day of wandering around. Bill headed off, with a burp, to the antiques markets, and I answered with my own belch, to take the Underground to the Tower of London.

I thought that I'd do a little people watching, and stand in the queue for the ticket window at Victoria Station's tube stop, rather than taking the possibly more expedient measure of purchasing a tube pass at a ticket machine. I'm not sure why more people don't step up to the ticket machines to purchase their tickets, but there are two possibilities that come to my mind. One: the ticket machines don't always function. Two: I get the impression that Londoners appreciate their downtime to just stand, rather than sprinting from point to point.

My purpose of standing in this line, for people watching, was uneventful aside from spotting a handsome woman a few people ahead of me in the queue. Well, I thought it was a woman. This person was impeccably dressed, in a becoming outfit with an alluring hat, gloves, and purse as accessories. My gosh, on further look this person was a man. I think. Maybe this was a large-boned woman with manly features wearing make-up done just so. I'll never know, and that's ok.

I had my turn at the ticket window, and purchased an all day pass for the inner two zones of London, and headed to the Circle Line.

The Circle Line underground train, which would take me to the Tower Hill Station had on board a group of six-year-olds out for a field trip. One tyrant of a young girl kept poking her head into a little boy's mouth, telling him to "spit it out." Whatever the kid had in his mouth, he hid it well, as I never saw anything fly out of his mouth, even during the ten minutes that our train stood still in the depths of London and the kids grew more and more restless. Could they be on their way to the Tower of London for a field trip? I supposed so, as that was the direction that we were traveling in.

Long ago, when I was a kid in school, we took field trips to a fish hatchery, to the local post office, and to a dam. Once, we went to a zoo. I never would have imagined going to the Tower of London for a field trip. Those are lucky little bastards that live in London.

While we were waiting for the stalled train to get moving again, a Middle Eastern woman turned on a cassette player to let her fellow tube passengers appreciate her music. The tape player was turned to full volume, and had a rattling, tinny loudspeaker which didn't help the drone of her dissonance any too well. The woman walked around the car, requested donations for her cause, received some money from her passing acquaintances, turned off her cacophony and sat back down. The train lurched forward.

I departed the tube at the Tower Hill Station, and so did that group of youngsters. I was followed close behind by the boisterous group of six-year-olds. Rats. If I hurried, maybe I could get well ahead of them once inside the gates of the Tower.

A quick journey through a pedestrian tunnel led me to a view of what I had come to see: the Tower of London. I turned left, and headed toward the main street that looked as if it would lead me to the entrance. The main path was not exactly filled with pedestrians, but there were several other people walking along the pavement. Noticing a garden path with absolutely no one walking on it, I thought that would be a nice way to walk to the Tower. Though it was November, the grass was a deep, healthy green, many of the trees still had their leaves still in full swing, and flowers were blooming. I walked nearer to the River Thames, and at one point, not far from where one would begin to cross the Tower Bridge, I realized that I was taking the long way around. I was taking the really long way around.

Ten minutes earlier, when I passed though the pedestrian tunnel, I should have taken a right, rather than a left. I retraced my steps, not enjoying the garden path quite so much on this second pass through it. Twenty minutes later I was getting closer to the entrance of the Tower of London. Looking around, I noticed that, even given my detour, the short-legged field trippers were still well in back of me. I pressed on, taking advantage of my lead in the race.

A small slowdown occurred while I waited at the gate to get in. There weren't many people in line in front of me; in fact, it was a group of only three other foreigners, but they were having a little difficulty in figuring out the English monetary system.

After paying my entrance fee, £11.00, I believe it was (a little steep for a skinflint like me was my first opinion), I entered inside and ventured past the ancient walls. I discovered the Tower of London to be excellent, and worth the admission price, no matter how much was charged.

From the entrance at the twin-peaked Middle Tower, one walks along a causeway, across the moat, which is, for the time being, dry. The moat was drained in 1830 because of a foul stench that wasn't letting up; not surprisingly, a good amount of human bones were discovered in the moat at that time. I understand there are plans underway to fill the moat up again, presumably with water, and maybe (I hope) just a bone or two for old times' sake. The drawbridge is gone, but the causeway leads into the Byward Tower, where a portcullis, a gate and another portcullis are there to offer a cheery "Welcome in!"

I had read about the Yeoman Warder tours, which leave on regular schedules, and I wanted to be part of one of them. The Yeoman Warders are the guardians of the Tower, and actually have residences within the walls of the Tower. They are also known as Beefeaters, and there are arguments made about the origin of the Beefeater sobriquet, and whether it's disparaging or not. The name likely derives, of course, from the Yeoman Warders eating beef; some say it is because of a collective fondness for roast beef, others say that the lower classes jeered the guards because these poorer folks couldn't afford to eat meat.

Looking at a sign, I saw that the next Yeoman Warder tour was a quarter of an hour away, and a small crowd was beginning to gather for it. Rather than wait around, I started out on a self-guided tour in the general area of the starting point of the official tour. I dug my brochure from my pocket, and the first item that caught my eye was "How the Tower was protected against attack." I looked around, and spotted the closed circuit television cameras peeking out of the old walls. I supposed that must have been what the brochure was talking about.

After some aimless strolling around, I checked my watch, and realized the guided tour was due to begin within minutes.

CHAPTER THIRTEEN

The Tower of London

The Yeoman Warder tour at the Tower of London drew a crowd on the comfortably small side. There were around two dozen of us tourists on hand for the tour, and I noticed that the dress was casual. Some of the attire that I spotted was really on the casual side. I can understand wanting to be comfortable while touring London, but sweat pants? There was a group who had made it a point to really dress down for the tour, in togs that might be more suited to watching a Sunday football game at home, scratching at their privates, and drinking cheap canned beer.

As I was to discover, this was an American family who decided to not at least dig out some loose-fitting jeans for their vacation. Their nationality became apparent shortly after we began our tour, as the largest wallydraigle asked the Yeoman Warder his first smart aleck question. The tour guide mentioned a rope that holds a certain portcullis in place is centuries old but assured us that the rope should last a few more years. Mr. Sweat Pants mulled this over for several minutes, and we were well on to another part of the tour when Mr. Sweat Pants blurted out,

"How do you know how long that rope will last until those gates drop down?"

"What's that?" The tour guide questioned.

The Sweat Pants family had a chuckle over the great wit that seemed to part of their family heritage.

"How do you know," Mr. Sweat Pants countered, "that the rope won't break anytime and send the portercull-, portuh-, pormer- those bars coming down?"

"The rope is thick and strong, and has lasted centuries. It shouldn't be fraying soon."

"But how do you know that?"

The entire tour group was looking at this man, many with mouths opened wide, and probably thinking what I was thinking, "Shut up, change into real clothes, go home, and while you're at it, trim your beard and get a haircut."

The Yeoman Warder gazed at this fellow for a few long seconds, and replied that there has been no scientific testing done on the quality of the rope, but it is an English rope, and still looks good and strong. This wasn't an overwhelmingly witty response, but it broke the tension, and drew a chuckle from the crowd, as the Yeoman Warder herded us to our following sights. Mr. Sweat Pants was fairly silent for the rest of the tour, although he made several off-hand comments quietly to his family, who always nodded, smirked, and looked with loathing at our tour guide.

Our Yeoman Warder was a strong-looking man, with light blue eyes, a raven-beaked nose, a close-cropped grey beard, and large roll of fat which snuck up between his jacket collar and his chin. He seemed a fair, but stern man, with a bit of a limp, which he helped alleviate by use of a cane. Why anyone would have a gripe against this man is beyond me.

He told our group of the two young princes that were murdered inside the Bloody Tower in the year 1483; one suffocated with a pillow, the other stabbed to death. Their bodies were buried amongst rubble in the Bloody Tower's basement, and then reburied at a later time near to the White Tower, where they seemed to be forgotten about until 1674, when their skeletons were discovered, whereupon the King decreed that the boys' bones were to be relocated to Westminster Abbey.

Our group learned of the Lion Tower. This is where the Royal Menagerie was housed in the days of Henry I. Starting with a pride of lions, the menagerie grew to include leopards, a white bear, and an elephant. The menagerie was transferred to Regents Park in the early 1800's as the start of the London Zoo. The Lion Tower is no more.

Our Yeoman Warder showed us the other highlights of the grounds, including Traitor's Gate where the accused and sentenced prisoners would enter the Tower, the White Tower which is the oldest building on the site (well past its nine-hundredth year), and the Tower Green where beheadings occurred.

Here, at the Tower Green, our tour guide gave a nearly blow by blow description of Margaret Pole's execution in 1541. Margaret Pole was the Countess of Galisbury and a reluctant prisoner, who had decided in her final minutes not to be beheaded after all. This poor woman, past her 70th birthday, freed herself, jumped to and fro, sprinted about the green, and had appendages sliced at by the executioner's ax before she was finally brought to her demise. As the guide told this gory and animated history, a fair skinned woman standing not more than five feet to my right gasped at every detail, put her hand to her mouth, and began to gag. This fellow tourist had turned paler than she already was, and she just about lost her breakfast right then and there. As we moved on, she had to have support from her companions, as her legs were on the wobbly side. The history of the Tower of London is not for the faint of heart or those prone to nervousness.

Luckily for her, our next and final stop was at the Chapel Royal of St. Peter ad Vinsula (St. Peter in Chains), where we had a chance to sit down and rest ourselves after walking for the past three quarters of an hour, as our Yeoman Warder wound down his tour.

Outside, back on the Green, I heard American voices complaining about the length of the tour. It seems the last time they were in London they took this same tour, and it lasted a full hour, not fifty minutes. They said they felt cheated. I looked over, and, surprisingly, saw that these people were not wearing sweatpants.

The rest of midday was spent doddering around the Tower grounds. I was about to have a look to see how long the line was to get in to see the Crown Jewels, but there was a group of pre-adolescent field-trippers vociferating and galloping towards the Waterloo Block, where the Crown Jewels are kept, and I thought that there might just be a quieter time to check out the situation after seeing a few other pieces of history on the grounds.

This pack of vocal children did make me wonder whatever happened to the group with which I had had my footrace a little earlier. There were a lot of school groups here, and I spotted several unruly mobs of youngsters before recognizing my adversaries. They were walking in one direction, and I quickly turned in the opposite direction, and made my tracks to the White Tower, never to lay eyes upon them again.

The White Tower was constructed between the years 1078 and 1097. It received its white coloring in 1241 when the stones that make up the building were whitewashed. This tremendous building is ninety feet high, and the walls are fifteen feet thick at the base, narrowing to a slender almost eleven feet wide towards the upper heights. To get inside, one takes the long, wooden steps to the south entry. The Tower was built with no doors on the ground level and only one doorway on the southern side of the structure.

Inside is where the kings of England lived in medieval days. Today, the Royal Armories are displayed, with antique weaponry and suits of armor (including the jumbo-sized 1500's armor of Henry VIII, and a small child's armor, which stands only three feet high). The chopping block and axe are there, and are the actual ones that were employed on the Tower Green. The chopping block is filled with the indentations and ruts of many cut marks on its top, but one cut mark is deepest. That is the one that the executioners would aim for in practice and in actual beheadings.

I was fortunate enough to be at the Tower when an exhibit from the Public Records Office was on display inside the White Tower. The center-piece of the attraction was the *Domesday Book*, which was on display behind glass. The *Domesday Book* was a survey ordered in 1086 by William the Conqueror; he wanted to know just how much he could tax the populace of England. Ol' William sent legali to have a chat with everyone in his domain to find out how much land, livestock, and other possessions they had, and in the meantime the request was made by his officers (quite politely, I'm sure) for an oath of allegiance to Mr. Conqueror. The taxes that were levied by the legali were irrevocable, and probably were the doomsday for at least a few of the people of England.

This was an interesting book to behold, but what really caught my eye was the part of the exhibit that contained a mummified rat, also under protective glass. This little guy had had a busy life, gnawing away at all kinds of good stuff, and he looked serene and happy in his duty of being a really old specimen of an English rat.

Elsewhere, I spied a passageway that seemed to be causing a great deal of mirth for those exiting the room behind the door. I had to have a look, too. Up a few steps I found a medieval toilet. It was a small room, with a hole in the stones where one could, in years past, let one's excre-ment drop down onto the ground outside the walls of the building. Rats and shit. Do the good old days get any better than this?

Exiting the White Tower, I walked back around to the Waterloo Block, which looked fairly quiet. I surmised that this could be an oppor-tune time to have a peek at the Crown Jewels. I'd hate to try having a look at these things on a busy day. There is an enormous queuing area, which I imagine is filled with sightseers during the peak season. As it was, it took only a few minutes of standing in line, then I realized that the line wasn't really a queue at all, but a bunch of people mesmerized by a film of the queen sitting down and waving. I strode past and went right into the exhibit.

The Crown Jewels were interesting to have a look at, but I wouldn't waste too much time standing in line to see a bunch of fancy stuff like this. Some people are awed by the splendor (the orb, the swords, the scepters, the gold and silver plates, and the crowns); I think they're dandy, but, even given the historical significance of all these prized doo-dads, I would say that I've seen them once, that was enough for me. Besides, I was ready for a snack.

I found a stand inside the Tower's walls that sold a host of mesmerizing choices. I looked at the opportunities to stuff my belly: sandwiches, cakes, biscuits, packages of crisps…everything looked good. I looked at the prices being charged, and decided that a packet of crisps would tide me over until I found something elsewhere more reasonably priced.

Munching my bag of crisps, I had a look at the area where the Tower's ravens call home. I had noticed a raven or two earlier, and had heard that they have their wings clipped lest they fly away, which will, of course, lead to White Tower crumbling, and the downfall of England. I felt sorry for these big black birds. They do look like they are making an earnest attempt to escape into flight, but their flapping wings only send them in a small circle, and they're never really able to lift far off the ground. There are warning signs around not to get too close to the ravens, as they may be dangerous. I'd be dangerous, too, if I were one of them. However, they are well cared for. They're probably just a little ill at ease because they're not able to do the flying that nature intended them to do.

Oh, well. After these thoughts of ravens, I had finished my bag of crisps. I threw the crumpled up litter into a bin, and walked though the Medieval Palace and along the walls of the Tower, where I took in a sweeping look at the grounds and persuaded a fellow tourist to snap a picture of me. I decided I had had enough of the Tower of London for this visit, although it was imperative that I take a stroll through the gift shop. I was glad I did, as I found a nice little cast metal block and axe knickknack to purchase.

CHAPTER FOURTEEN

An Afternoon Rambling about London

The Tower Bridge is a short few minutes' walk from the Tower of London, and has an exhibition called the Tower Bridge Experience. I was tempted to pay for a tour, which includes short movies about the bridge's history, a stroll along the catwalk 150 feet above the Thames, and a peek inside the bridge's engine room. (The Tower Bridge is a bascule bridge, opening for large ships that pass underneath it.) I decided that the tour would most likely be wonderful and informative, but the time was already past one o'clock, and I was thinking that I might just want to take in at least a couple other areas of the city before the sun set; the November nightfall was only three hours away.

I did have a walk half ways across the eight hundred foot long Tower Bridge (just on the main level, not on the lofty catwalk) to have a look up and down the Thames and to be at least partially transpontine. It's a good view, with blue water that stretches out for a distance.

In the 19th century, when indoor plumbing was gaining popularity, sewage would discharge straight into the Thames, and the river was an expansive open cesspit with a putrid odor. The last straw came one summer in mid-century, when rainfall was limited and the odor from the river became more prevalent as the summer wore on. The Members of Parliament found that their work was impossible to perform, as the smell permeated the Houses of Parliament. (Never mind that the fish that lived in the river had been disappearing from the pollution and that people had died from cholera, now the MP's were being inconvenienced!) In 1864 work was begun on a sewage system, and water from the River Thames is now depended on by millions of people, and it is considered to be one of the cleanest urban rivers in the world. And the fish are back.

There are river cruises that a person can take on the Thames. A shorter, half-hour cruise might not have been a bad way to while away some time. Looking up the river, I spotted St. Paul's Cathedral off in the distance, and I was reminded by the site that I had better stop dwelling on the scenery, as I had to continue on with my sightseeing.

I was momentarily fascinated by Dead Man's Hole, just off the bridge. This is where corpses, which had been tossed out of the Tower, were retrieved. The bodies were stored in a mortuary just steps away until they were buried.

Before I got on the Tube to St. Paul's Cathedral, I decided to have a look around the dock area. I discovered an upscale section of London called St. Katherine's Dock, which boasts a big, fancy hotel, posh shops, and yacht slips. This is definitely not the type of place that I would have decided on as a destination, but it was a nice diversion. I stopped into a shop to pick up a postcard and a snack. The postcard features an old Guinness toucan advertisement and reads "Lovely Day for a Guinness," a sentiment with which I heartily agree, and the snack was a 9 to 5 Bar. The bar was good, with a yummy combination of ingredients including oats, apple jam, and chocolate. I was energized and ready to head on to St. Paul's.

Looking at the Underground map in the Tower Hill Station, I grew a little perplexed about which direction I should set myself in for the most direct route to the cathedral. Both the District Line and the Circle Line westward bound would take me to Monument Station, where it looked like I'd have a bit of an underground walk to get to Bank Station, where I'd transfer to the Central Line, and at that point, the St. Paul's stop was only moments away to the west. Or, I could take the Circle Line north to the Liverpool Street Station, where I'd transfer to the Central Line west, past Bank Station, and depart the train at the St. Paul's stop.

This is where, I decided, that the information booths in the stations come in handy. I noticed that the information booth attendant was looking slightly bored, and needed someone to confuse. I was there to liven up her day. I posed my two alternatives to her about which way would be the most efficient way to travel to St. Paul's Cathedral. She didn't have to take a second to mull my query over. The best way to St. Paul's, according to the attendant, was to take the District Line or the Circle Line westward, and depart at the Mansion House Station. From there, I would have only a couple blocks' walk to St. Paul's Cathedral.

Now that was not the answer that I expected. I hadn't considered that alternative at all. In my dumfounded state, I asked her to repeat the directions again, slowly, so I would be able to remember them. With a gracious smile, and the personality of a rock, she repeated the directions. I repeated to myself, "Mansion House, Mansion House, Mansion House." That stop didn't sound familiar in the slightest way.

I stopped to have a look at an Underground map on the station wall. I spotted Mansion House, which appeared to be far south from where I wanted to end up. There must have been some misunderstanding about where I wanted to go to on the tube. Perhaps the attendant misunderstood "St. Paul's Cathedral," and thought that I had said "Mansion House." At any rate, the Mansion House stop looked to be at least a half-mile from the St. Paul's stop, and all that extra traipsing around would cut too much time out of my busy afternoon.

I decided to take my first choice of a route. I entered a westbound train, and got off at the next stop, which was Monument Station. From there I took a series of escalators, hallways, and staircases to more hallways, always following the signs that directed me towards the Bank Station. Once there, I waited patiently for the next Central Line train going north. I looked at a map on the station wall and gauged the distance between the Bank Station and the St. Paul's stop. I guessed that it couldn't be more than one or two blocks, and I thought about exiting the Bank Station and walking the final distance. A lighted sign was announcing that my train was still several minutes away; I could probably walk to the cathedral before the train even gets to this station.

I remembered then, that the Underground maps are not drawn to scale. They are drawn to make it easy to read them. I waited for the train, thanking my memory for kicking in and saving me who knows how much walking. And, as I had time for pondering, the thought of traveling to the Mansion House Station would have been ludicrous; that attendant was either misunderstanding me or she was deliberately attempting to get me lost. I snorted, and noticed one or two other people waiting for the train step back from me after mature consideration.

Now, this may be a little difficult to believe, but it didn't dawn on me that since the Underground maps are not drawn to scale (this was Harry Beck's design, back in 1931, and it has stuck), that the cathedral really could be only a couple blocks away from the Mansion House stop, and the attendant was absolutely correct. I didn't realize that until oh… until about two paragraphs back, when I pulled out a London map to refresh my memory on the Tube Station names. I got to thinking; maybe I should see where that Mansion House stop really is in relation to St. Paul's Cathedral. They *are* about two blocks apart from each other, and I would have had a direct route if I had taken the tube from the Tower Hill Station to Mansion House, rather than all my walking underground between stations and transferring lines.

As it was, I made it to the St. Paul's stop without further delay, and the St. Paul's stop really is convenient to the Cathedral, but it seems to be most convenient if you are already on the Central Line to begin with.

I was sure that I was less than a block away from the Cathedral, but I didn't see it. I decided that it must be just a little ways up the street, so I turned up Newgate Street, and saw that a new building was being constructed that required a thorough walking around. I turned onto Warwick Lane, impressed by the size of the construction site, but not spying St. Paul's Cathedral anywhere around. Nearing Ludgate Hill, I spotted the Cathedral. I had, indeed, walked in exactly the wrong direction to get to the Cathedral, but in the process, I was fortunate to see some of London's newest construction taking place.

The St. Paul's that we know of today is actually the fourth cathedral on the site. The first was built of wood, in the year 604, and burnt down after some sixty-odd years. A new cathedral, which took the burnt one's place, was ransacked and wrecked by the Vikings after a life of three hundred years. The replacement, "Old St. Paul's", lasted until the Great Fire of 1666. Incidentally, it was at Old St. Paul's that the foot of the statue of St. Algar was measured, giving us our twelve-inch standard of measurement. The modern-day St. Paul's Cathedral had its foundation laid in 1675, thirty-three years later the domed masterpiece was completed.

The many steps leading up to the west porch of St. Paul's were covered with people, mostly college-aged it seemed, who were studying, contemplating, or napping. It's a domino effect, I know. One act can certainly lead to the next one. I walked up the steps, into the main entrance, thinking that it would be nice to spend a quiet hour in here, admiring the massive arches, saucer-like domes, intricate carvings, mosaics on the ceilings, and the Whispering Gallery. I had a peek inside the nave, and thought that this would well worth the £5.00 admission charge. Looking at my watch, though, I saw that the time was already past three o'clock, and I hadn't had lunch yet. I was ready for food. My 9 to 5 bar had worn off some time ago.

I had heard of a small restaurant in the lower section of St. Paul's. Going out the doorway, back out onto the west porch, and down the steps I made a half-hearted bid to find the café in the crypt, but before I did too much searching, I saw a place across the way called Enough 2 Feed an Elephant. Eating in an old underground graveyard would be interesting, but I was of the opinion that I was ready for food as immediately as I could find it, and as far as I was concerned, my search was over.

I looked though the selection of plastic-wrapped sandwiches, and decided on an egg roll (an egg salad and watercress sandwich made with white bread), and a small pot of tea. Taking a seat by a window, I admired the perseverance of a young couple, around twenty years of age, attempting to eat at an outside table. The sun was out, but dusk was beginning to set in; the wind was starting to whip around and the air was getting a bit on the chilly side. Still, the couple ate, shared a cigarette, and laughed, making attempts to fend off birds whose appetites had perked up, which caused the couple to laugh even more. The couple didn't seem to have a care in the world. I was enjoying my sandwich, and the tea made a nice rounding-out of my lunch as I looked out the window, watching the show.

A strong gust of wind blew though the cracks in the building, sending the smoke from the couple's cigarette wafting into the building. It was a sweet smell, which smelled awfully pleasant; I finally grasped that the large hand-rolled cigarette wasn't tobacco, but an honest to goodness joint of a magnitude that would make any marijuana enthusiast proud. I wasn't the only one that caught on to this scent of ganja. One of the girls who was working behind the counter at the restaurant marched outside to have a talk with these two kids. It looked to be a polite discussion, and they ended their talk with the counter girl smiling, taking a mighty drag from the cigarette, wishing the couple well, and going back to work.

I was done with my lunch, and the couple outside was leaving (not only leaving their table, but also leaving their trash behind as they threw everything full force towards the litter bin, but missed it by a good several feet, and left their mess to blow around in the wind). It was time for me to leave, too.

CHAPTER FIFTEEN

"You Must Not Be From England!"

Tired, and full from my late lunch, I considered going back to the B&B, but I thought better of it. I briefly weighed my inclination of going to Old Bailey to see how the scales of the justice system were doing, but it was rather late in the afternoon; I surmised that Old Bailey might be closing its doors for the day before long.

There was still enough time left in London to have a look at some of the exhibits in the British Library, and I was near there, so why not?

Before leaving on this trip to England, I had answered questions about what I had planned to see and to do. The British Library was near the top of my list of stuff to do. The mention of visiting a library on a vacation was far from everyone's minds. I was given alternatives from several individuals. "Stay out all night and go to the punk rock clubs." "Spend a day in the Houses of Parliament and become familiar with the British political system." "Start drinking at pubs in the morning, and don't let up at any time." "See the magnificence and splendor of Buckingham Palace." "England? Why England? I'd go to Mexico instead and get drunk for a week!" "I wouldn't go on a vacation; I'd do something more practical, like fix up my house. Once you take a vacation it's gone and you have nothing to show for it."

Well, I've always liked libraries, and the British Library is suggested to be one of the finest in the world, and I wanted to see it, no matter what anyone else thought of my plans. Besides, I did want to have a gander at the original Beatles lyrics that were displayed in a gallery.

Before I knew it, I was on the Central Line to Oxford Circus, where I transferred north to the Euston Station. Once I was off the tube I went…in the wrong direction. MAN! How do I manage to do that? After asking a well-dressed woman, who looked like she knew exactly where she was marching to, if she knew the way to the British Library, she told me, "Sorry." She said that she was a little turned around, also, as she had gotten off her bus at the wrong stop, and she wasn't sure where she was, either. At least that was her story.

I walked along further, before it set in that I was, indeed, not heading in the direction which might be considered the most direct route to the library.

Going back towards Euston Station, I asked a couple of men in suits if they could direct me towards the library.

"The *British* Library?" one of them asked me.

"Yes. The British Library."

They gestured me on my way, and I thanked them.

The British Library was several blocks in the direction that I originally didn't turn in. I found a large red brick building with almost the look of a large, nearly windowless shopping center. In the post 4 PM darkness, I walked across the piazza to the entrance, picked up a brochure, and looked around to decide which way to turn.

My focal point of visiting the British Library was the John Ritblat Gallery. Sir John Ritblat, a fairly well-off gent employed by the British Land Company, donated one million pounds to the library in order to buy and install display cabinets for the gallery which was to take on his name. The gallery is subtitled *Treasures of the British Library* and is a remarkable room, filled with valued articles of years gone by.

Walking around the gallery, which had few other visitors when I was there, led me to a book of Aesop's Fables from the 14th century, Beowulf from the 11th century, an original Alice In Wonderland with drawings by the author Lewis Carroll, Bach scores, and scores by Mozart, as well. Beethoven's tuning fork was there, as were drawings by Leonardo da Vinci, and Bibles from the olden days (the 800's). A person can read over the death warrant of the Earl of Essex, signed off with zeal by Elizabeth the First in 1601. The old items were interesting, but what drew me to the library in the first place was that collection of Beatles memorabilia.

A nice display of original lyrics was in this exhibit. "I Want To Hold Your Hand," "Fool on the Hill," "A Hard Day's Night," "Strawberry Fields" among several other lyrics were behind glass, with lines crossed out, and new words scribbled in on all the pieces of paper. I spent a while attempting to decipher the handwriting on the crossed out lines of the familiar tunes before moving on. I had a listen in the public headphones to bits of the National Sound Gallery: Florence Nightingale gave a speech, an Indian bird sang in the first recording ever of a non-human, and the Beatles said hello. I was wondering how many ears those headphones had clamped onto. Plenty, I'm sure. There was another audio-enthusiast at the headphones right next to me. Given the aroma emitting from him, I expect that ear hygiene wasn't at the top of his list of stuff to do. I gulped, and moved on again. Up an escalator, I spied a room advertising rare books. The guard, however, chased me away. I didn't have a pass. A little more rambling around, then I had had my fill and walked back to Euston Station. A man with an open guitar case, strumming a guitar, and singing his heart out earned a few coins from myself and several other passersby in the Euston tube station, and I hopped on the Underground to take me to Victoria Station.

The Victoria Line makes its connection from Euston Station to Victoria Station with stops at Warren Street, Oxford Circus and Green Park. I was happy not to have to make a transfer. Walking back to the Georgian House Hotel, I decided to stop into a pub that I had passed by on many trips to and from the bed and breakfast. A half-pint of ale would suit me just right after a busy day.

Given my American manner of saying "half", which the English seemed to have a hard time comprehending, I asked the bartender for a "hoff" pint of Guinness, in an attempt to make his job a little easier. I had noticed over the past several days that my Midwestern dialect was seeming a little strange each time I opened my trap; I seemed to have some sort of nasally intonation to my voice, and I was pronouncing words just a little wrong, so I was happy to finally realize how to ask for my half pint of Guinness.

"You must not be from England!" the bartender expressed when I placed my order with him.

"No, I'm not." I countered with my flat nasally whine, "I'm from the States. Minnesota to be exact."

"You know how I knew you weren't from around here?"

"No. How?" I was growing thirsty for my stout, and the bartender had yet to begin pouring it, and I was growing just a little edgy.

"None of the local people order Guinness. It's only the foreigners that order Guinness. That's how I knew. You should really try a local ale."

I appreciated his candor. Any other time I would have taken him up on his guidance to discover a local London-made brew, but I really had my heart set on a Guinness, and I was not about to be swayed in a different direction.

"I've enjoyed many of the different English beers over the past week, and I've liked several of them, but for right now, I'd just like a half pint of Guinness. It's been a long day, I'm flying back to Minnesota tomorrow, and I need to be on my way soon to meet someone."

The bartender pulled out a half-pint glass from underneath the bar, and held the glass in his hands.

"I'll bet you've seen all the tourist attractions around London."

"Some." I said with haste.

"I never go out and see the historical sights. I grew up knowing that they are around, but I never actually see them."

The moment had still not arrived when he would begin to draw my beer, and this man was beyond the point of beginning to antagonize me. I was about to offer him a piece of my mind when he decided to confirm that it was a Guinness which I had requested. I replied with a faint-hearted affirmation. He finally poured my beer; I paid for it, and I downed it in two quick gulps. I immediately turned and headed out the door to get away from the bartender as quickly as possible.

Sputtering to myself about the lack of genuine customer care in the pub that I was in, I got lost in my inner fuming, and also in the neighborhood streets, and that didn't make me in any better of a mood. I traipsed the blocks a few times before I finally found the bed and breakfast.

Inside the Georgian House and back in our room, I spotted a bottle of Guinness in the waste bin and the smell of Indian food in the air. Bill had gotten back to the Georgian House not long before me. He had picked up an order of Chicken Balti and garlic nan for £2.30 from the Spicy Hot Indian Takeaway, and he was relaxing on his bed watching a television program after finishing his meal.

We talked about our various excursions throughout the day. Bill had, for the most part, taken in various markets, although he had visited St. Paul's Cathedral just a half-hour before I had been there, and decided on the same course of action, which was to have a quick look inside, then move on.

I had a quick rest. We agreed that we had to do a little grocery shopping at Tesco. Tesco is a grocery store chain with a good selection of the necessities. My necessities for bringing back home, I decided once we were at Tesco, were packets of bread pudding mix, Yorkshire pudding mix, shepherd's pie mix, and a tube of Colman's mustard, along with a few other light and easy to transport items. I drew the line at buying a tin of sliced luncheon tongue, but I found it necessary to pick up a tin of a full English breakfast. This 415 gram canned breakfast, called "All Day Breakfast" contains beans, sausages, pork, chopped egg nuggets, bacon, and mushrooms, all swimming in tomato sauce. It was too tempting to pass by.

Then it was on to the Country Pub for supper. I enjoyed a couple pints of Guinness poured by an accommodating bartender, with a bowl of sausages and greens. The sausages were thinly sliced, with toothpicks poking into several of them, and the greens were... maybe kale? I'm not sure. Bill was still full from his supper earlier, but he ordered a pint of Guinness, also, along with garlic bread, which had almost as much bread as garlic, from my tastes of it (just the way it should be).

Back at the B&B, the Italian girls in the room next door were once again having a difficult time trying to get to sleep. Tonight they also seemed to have some problem attempting to lock their door as the hour grew late. BAM! Shut. Open. BAM! Shut. Open. BAM! Shut. And so on it went. They shouted to the front desk for assistance, and seemed amazed to discover that it was so easy to lock their door. I have no idea how many times I heard these girls slam that door, but it took a long time to get to sleep that night.

Epilogue

I decided to be bold for breakfast and include the hotel's tomato offering in my full English breakfast plan. I've never been that enthused about tomatoes, to the surprise of all that think they are a wonderful food, but I'll put up with them. I had the full course, and included was a whole, raw tomato, sliced in two. A little hard, and not the best tomato I've tried. The rest of the breakfast made up for that, though. I was tired after the long week and the previous night's restless sleep.

We caught the Gatwick Express from Victoria Station. Bill had his return trip ticket, and I purchased my ticket for the ride to Gatwick from the conductor.

It was a packed train and Bill and I sat across from each other. Once the train got moving, I mentioned to Bill that I was ready for a good, greasy pizza once I was home, as I had missed my traditional Friday night pizza on our trip. This opened up the lines of communication from a man and woman who were seated next to us. They overheard my comment about the pizza, and this couple, from Arkansas as it turned out, talked about their four-day trip to London, including spending two hours to wait for the changing of the guard the day before at Buckingham Palace. Once the time came for the changing of the guard, they could hardly see the action. This was so tiring for them that they had to go back to their bed and breakfast to rest up.

They were nice folks, and were genuinely excited about the vacation they took, but they seemed to have had a little too much downtime on their trip to England, and I could have used a little more resting and little less conversing on this train ride.

But, we talked about how busy London is, and how crowded the Underground is when everyone is going to work. I mentioned that I live in a small suburb just north of Minneapolis, and I think there's a lot of traffic when I have to wait for four cars to pass at a street on my way to work. "Well, I've got you beat there!" the man said. He was on to a diatribe about how his town was smaller than my town. Without a fight, I let him win.

There was a bit of a wait at Gatwick; Bill and I passed the time by buying a few odds and ends from an airport store to take home, then sitting down and reading. Like a sentence out of the second to the last closing paragraph from a book, our friends from Arkansas walked by, smiled, and waved.

Once on the plane, we waited an hour on the tarmac before taking off. The airline gave us a filling meal somewhere over the Atlantic: roast beef, mashed potatoes, fruit, a roll with clotted cream, and a glass of wine. It was a good meal, but not quite as satisfying as a full English breakfast.

About the Author

Todd Wisti has spent the better part of his years writing, in one fashion or another. As a bass player for various rock'n'roll ensembles over a twelve year period (including the Minneapolis based bands *The Masterbeats* and *The Landsliders*), he wrote and co-wrote pop songs for the unsuspecting but forgiving public. His attention turned towards creative nonfiction at North Hennepin Community College, after receiving an award and placement of a short story in the college's quarterly magazine.

Born in Oroville, California, he now calls Columbia Heights, Minnesota his home.

Bibliography and Internet Resources

Boulware, Jack. "London Calling." *Travelocity Magazine, N.p., N.d.*

Bowen, Angela and Susie Hirschfield (editors). *Britain.* British Tourist Authority, 2000

Bryson, Bill. *Notes from a Small Island.* William Morrow and Company, 1995

Darlington & Stockton Times. November 10, 2000

"Domesday Book." *Encarta.* Microsoft, 1997

Durden-Smith, Jo. "Liquid Asset." *Expedia Travels.* November/December 2000: 128–136

Hanson, Neil (editor). *1987–1988 The Best Pubs of Great Britain.* The East Woods Press, 1986

Herriot, James. *All Things Bright and Beautiful.* St.Martin's Press, 1974

James Herriot's Yorkshire. St. Martin's Press, 1979

James Herriot's Yorkshire Revisted. St. Martin's Press, 1999

Heritage Wales. Total Wales Media and Marketing, 2000

Leapman, Michael. *London.* Dorling Kindersley Limited, 1997

Levine, Dan and Richard Jones. *Frommer's Walking Tours: England's Favorite Cities*. Prentice Hall, 1994

London Planner. MFA Publications, March 2000

Neillands, Rob, Ross Finlay, Roger Thomas, Terence Sheehy. *Journey Through Britain and Ireland*. Fraser Stewart Book Wholesale Ltd., 1992

Road Atlas of Great Britain. AA Publishing, 1995

Roberts, Andy. *Ghosts and Legends of Yorkshire*. Jarrold Publishing, 1992

Sandler, Corey. *Econoguide London*. Contemporary Books, 2000

Scott, John. "Feeling Walled In? Then Head for York." *Dalesman*. May 2001: 56-59

Steves, Rick. *Great Britain and Ireland 2000*. John Muir Publications, 2000

Straach, Kathryn. "Britain's City of York Thrives on the Past." *St. Paul Pioneer Press*, Sec F, N.d.

Toth, Susan Allen. *England for All Seasons*. Ballantine Books, 1997

"2001 Travellers' Choice Awards." *British Heritage*. April/May 2001: 48

Werner, Laurie. "Along the Thames." *Expedia Travels*. November/December 2000: 138–140

Wight, James. *The Real James Herriot: A Memoir of My Father*. Ballantine Books, 2000

Williams, Charles. *Cardiff 2000*. Cardiff Marketing, 1999

Willis, Monica Michael. "London's Flea Markets." *Country Living*. April 2001: 41–47

Wright, Peter. *Yorkshire Placenames*, Dalesman Publishing Company Limited, 2001

www.bl.uk (British Library)

www.ipl.org (Internet Public Library)

www.riverthames.co.uk (River Thames Guide)

www.tower-of-london.com (Tower of London)

www.york.gov.uk (City of York Council)

Yapp, Nick. *London: The Secrets and the Splendour.* Könemann Verlagsgesellschaft mbH, 1999

Index

CPSIA information can be obtained
at www.ICGtesting.com
Printed in the USA
FSOW01n2003090817
37431FS

9 780595 191963